The Requirements

The term 'Weapon System' came into vogue in the 1960s. The vehicle delivering the ordnance was supported by an infrastructure of maintenance support, training, armament procurement, front-line servicing and target identification processes which had been tailored to the needs of the vehicle and its role. There was nothing new in the concept for the navies of the world, for ever since ships had been built as warships the designers had been obliged to recognise the need for systematic design, striking a balance between the needs of propulsion, crew accommodation and compatibility with shore facilities (depth of water and size of slips or drydocks) while incorporating the best possible armament to carry out naval tasks.

The aircraft carrier added new difficulties to system design, the armament sub-system being no less complex than the ship on which it was imposed.

The basic requirements for a carrier are that it should be able to accommodate sufficient aircraft to carry out its intended role, that it should be able to fly off aircraft in all normal weather conditions, control them when airborne and then recover them safely. In addition to between-flight servicing, maintenance facilities to permit minor repairs and replacement of major items, such as engines and mainplanes, have to be provided in the form of various workshops – airframe, engine, instrument, radio and electrical – as well as stowage space for spares. Magazines must be provided for all the forms of ordnance likely to be needed by the aircraft – torpedoes, bombs, rocket projectiles, mines, gun ammunition and pyrotechnics – and this must be readily available at short notice but must be stowed well out of harm's way. Just as dangerous in its way is aviation fuel, of which large quantities must be stowed and which must be delivered to the aircraft through an elaborate fuel main system. Existing ships' facilities, such as command and control 'offices', communications, electrical supplies, fire-fighting capacity and, above all, personnel accommodation must be greatly expanded, all within a hull whose size is dictated by outside considerations.

Setting aside structural limitations and building slipway capacity, the size of any country's warships is limited by docking facilities – the length of the empty drydock and the width of the gates being critical. In effect, this limited the size of British ships to a length of 800ft (244m) and a beam of 97ft (29.5m), but with docks available in Gibraltar, Durban, Singapore and Sydney, the Royal Navy was nevertheless better able to conduct world-wide operations. Japan and America both possessed bigger docks, but after the former had isolated herself in the early '30s she had only those facilities in the Home Islands dockyards and those which could be acquired by conquests. The United States, isolationist since the First World War, had sufficient facilities for her naval needs, with good naval dockyards on both East and West Coasts, and also at Pearl Harbor, 2,100 miles west of San Francisco. Although the USA built up a 'Two-Ocean Navy', capable of conducting operations simultaneously in the Atlantic and Pacific, transfers between oceans were necessary and as the Panama Canal reduced the New York to Francisco voyage from 13,200 miles (round Cape Horn) to 5,200 miles it was essential that all warships should be able to pass through the Canal. The minimum width of the locks was 110ft, which imposed a maximum beam of about 108ft (33m) on ships intended to use the Canal; the length was sufficient for a 1,000-ft (305m) ship but design considerations restricted the waterline length of a ship of the maximum permissible beam to about 860ft. Britain and France, both with colonial possessions in the Pacific, also exercised conscious restraint on the size of their warships for these reasons, but the Japanese Navy was aware of that in time of war it had little chance of being granted permission to pass through the Canal (even if the strategic need existed) and therefore made no allowance for the Canal in warship design.

An artificial limit was also imposed upon aircraft carrier size by the various Naval Treaties between the World Wars. In 1922, the Washington Treaty limited the displacement tonnage of new construction to 23,000 tons, although permitting the completion of a few converted capital ships up to a maximum of 33,000 tons. On top of this limit on individual ships, there was an overall tonnage limitation – 135,000 tons for the USA and Britain, 83,000 tons for Japan and 54,000 tons for Italy and France. As will be seen, these restrictions led to some remarkable designs which were intended to beat the Treaties, particularly on the part of the Japanese, who contrived to produce an 8,000-ton 590-ft carrier capable of stowing 48 aircraft! Not until the end of 1936 were Treaty limits abandoned by Japan, and Britain remained tied by an Anglo-German Naval Agreement until 1939, so that the Royal Navy was armed throughout the War by ships designed under Treaty limits.

Aircraft Operating

In still air an aircraft will take off and land at speeds which are governed by its weight; for a given weight, the take-off rolling distance and speed will vary but little. The speed necessary is relative to the air, not to the ground, so that any wind blowing in the opposite direction to that in which the aircraft is taking off can be subtracted from the still-air take-off speed: an aircraft taking off at 85 knots Indicated Air Speed into a 20-knot wind will cover the distance needed to reach only 65 knots in still air. If the aircraft is then transferred to a ship steaming at 20 knots, it again needs to reach only 65 knots, and with 20 knots of wind in addition, this comes down to 45 knots, with a corresponding reduction in the take-off run. Landing is similarly affected by wind and ship speed, but the benefits are not a reduced landing run but added safety from a slow relative approach speed to a very limited landing area and lessened impact and deceleration forces on the air-frame.

Prior to WW2, the most usual method of launching aircraft from a carrier was to fly them off under their own power, the ship giving them the maximum available (and allowable) combined wind and ship speed ('wind over the deck') and take-off distance. Aircraft awaiting take-off were ranged right aft, but as the number of aircraft in the range was increased, so the available take-off distance was shortened, until the minimum safe run was reached. As the length of the run was variable, depending upon wind over the deck and aircraft weight, so the number of aircraft which could be ranged varied. The highest possible ship speed was therefore desirable, to compensate for any lack of wind, and most Fleet carriers built after 1925 were capable of attaining 28 knots or more under open sea conditions (as opposed to the 34 knots reached under trial conditions by some Japanese and American ships).

Between the wars, three British and two Japanese carriers were built to launch fighter aircraft from short flying-off decks at the level of the upper hangar deck, leaving the flight deck clear for landings and for launching strike aircraft. The increase in aircraft weights brought this practice to an end in the mid-'30s, the fighters becoming too heavy to get airborne in the short distance.

Devices for assisting take-off had been in general use aboard warships since the mid-'20s, primarily to launch seaplanes from capital ships and cruisers; the only early carriers to be so fitted were the first three American ships – *Langley, Lexington* and *Saratoga*. The catapults in these ships proved to be of little use as all the aircraft were capable of taking off with ease under most weather conditions. By the early '30s, aircraft weights and take-off speeds were increasing and the fourth American carrier, *Ranger*, was fitted with two improved pneumo-hydraulic catapults, capable of launching 7,000lb aircraft at up to 60 knots. This speed was relative to the deck and, known as the 'end speed', and was variable to allow for a range of aircraft weights – a 9,000lb aircraft being launched at 55 knots. Excessive take-off speed was avoided by reducing either the ship's speed or by reducing the catapult end speed (to a minimum of about 45 knots). The advantages of the catapult, apart from its ability to shoot aircraft off in conditions unfavourable for free take-off, were that it permitted a much larger number of aircraft to be ranged – the track occupying barely 100ft of the deck length – or permitted the remainder of the deck to be left free for other aircraft activities, such as maintenance, or re-organisation of the deck park. The disadvantages were that the launching cycle was such that only one aircraft could be launched per minute per catapult, as against one every ten seconds in a free take-off sequence aboard a well-drilled carrier, and the aircraft themselves required structural strengthening, involving additional weight, to stand up to the longitudinal acceleration.

The Royal Navy introduced an additional complication when *Glorious* and *Courageous* were fitted with 'accelerators' in 1935 and 1936. These ships were thus equipped to launch floatplanes (whose floats were stressed for deck landings), for which a launching trolley was employed. In order to provide commonality, the same trolley could be used to push a wheeled aircraft off, the forward

The first flat-top – HMS ARGUS *as she appeared when conducting flying trials after the end of the First World War. Points to note: The scuttles following the original sheer line of the cargo liner hull and the navigating position in the raised position.*
(GIEVES LTD)

struts providing the impetus while the rear struts held the aircraft in the flying attitude with its tail off the deck. The American catapult towed the aircraft into the air, a wire strop, called variously a 'bridle' or a 'pendant', connecting the aircraft to the moving shuttle of the catapult. The British trolley had collapsible legs and could quickly be stowed clear of the deck, but time was needed to adjust the length of the legs to suit different types of aircraft and the sheer weight of the trolley absorbed energy, so that the end speed of the accelerator at maximum aircraft weight was generally less than that provided by the catapult. A further disadvantage of the accelerator was that four attachment spools were needed on the aircraft to match the trolley legs; these spools had to project out from the aircraft's surface, whereas the two attachment hooks for the catapult bridle could be fitted in the wheel wells of retracting undercarriage aircraft, with an obvious saving in drag once the aircraft was airborne. During the war, British Accelerated Take-Off Gear (ATOG) was modified to permit the American-style tail-down towed launch method, with a consequent improvement in end speed/aircraft weight maxima.

The Japanese Navy, although adopting a German catapult design for its capital ships and cruisers, did not install catapults in its carriers. Japanese naval aircraft were generally lighter and had superior take-off performance to their Western contemporaries until 1943. Thereafter, the IJN was increasingly embarrassed by its lack of catapults, for the larger carriers which could have operated the heavier new aircraft had been greatly reduced in numbers and the Fleet was depending upon converted ships whose deck length was inadequate. Rocket-assisted take-off gear was developed and used to a limited degree, but in its last attempt to take on the US Navy in a carrier battle, the Imperial Japanese Navy was forced to deploy obsolescent aircraft aboard four carriers which were too small for the modern bomber types.

Rocket-assisted Take-off Gear (RATOG) was also used by the Royal Navy to a limited extent, primarily aboard American-built carriers whose catapults were not compatible with British aircraft fitted for ATOG launches. Employed to launch aircraft at high weights and/or in low relative wind speeds, the take-off run was at least as long as that taken in normal weight/wind conditions and the risk of not all the units firing or burnt-out units failing to release cleanly did not endear RATOG to the crews.

After some false starts the technique of landing aircraft on ships with the aid of arrester gear was established in all the interested navies by the early 1930s. The Royal Navy's first 'production model' arrester gear appeared in 1918 and reflected the concern lest an aircraft should be lost over the ship's side after touch-down. Parallel wires ran along the deck to be engaged by hooks on the aircraft axle – once firmly attached, the aircraft could not leave the deck again; in practice, the aircraft did not always attach itself firmly and the gear acquired a reputation for causing more deck-landing accidents than it prevented and for exacerbating the damage sustained in accidents for which it was not responsible. In spite of manifest shortcomings, the longitudinal arrester gear system was also adopted by the Japanese Navy for its first carrier (fitted out with the assistance of a British Naval Mission) and surprisingly, by the US Navy, which opted for a 'Belt and Braces' answer, using what was to become the conventional transverse arrester wire arrangement to stop the forward movement in conjunction with the fore-and-aft wires to stop movement in any other direction. By 1925, the Royal Navy had dispensed with its wires altogether and for the next eight years British aircraft relied upon a slow landing speed and the wind over the deck to remain on the deck and come to a stop. In the meantime, American, Japanese and French carriers were using 'self-rendering' arrester wires which allowed an aircraft to land off-centre and take a wire without the risk of swinging; while at the same time gradually centering itself relative to the deck. By the mid '30s, a typical arrester gear system could accept 8,000lb aircraft at up to 60 knots relative entry speed, imposing a 2g load on the aircraft in a 140ft maximum 'pull-out' distance. The number of wires available varied, but usually ranged between eight and ten in a Fleet carrier, spaced some 20 to 30ft apart, the aftermost being at least 100ft from the end of the deck in order to ensure that the aircraft passed well above the stern of the ship even in rough weather with the deck pitching heavily. The actual deceleration units – hydraulic in British and American ships and electric in Japanese carriers – were usually connected to two wires to save space and weight.

An excessively strong wind over the deck could be as much embarrassment as insufficient wind, preventing handling operations such as the manual folding or spreading of wings or even, in extreme cases, causing aircraft once landed to be lifted into the air again by a momentary gust. In such cases the conventional procedure was to steam the carrier astern, to *increase* the relative approach speed of the aircraft and reduce the wind over the deck. In the mid-1930s the US Navy decided to improve on this method by installing arrester wires forward, to recover aircraft over the bows in case of necessity. British Fleet carriers built after 1940 also featured

Contrasts in 'blunt ends': a Fulmar landing on HMS ILLUSTRIOUS *in November 1940 and a Hellcat at the 'Cut' over* INTREPID'S *ramp in May 1945. Note the British carrier's lift (below the Fulmar) marks the after end of the hangar whereas the 'Essex' class after lift was just abaft the island, the location of the countersunk 4.5-in turrets which narrowed the deck to less than 60 feet at the top of the round-down and the position of the American ship's superimposed 5-in turrets at the rear of the island. The biplanes on* ILLUSTRIOUS *starboard outrigger stowages are Gloster Sea Gladiator fighters.* (JDB & US NAVY)

wires forward, but the occasions for use were limited and by 1944 no further installations were planned for new classes of carrier. The disposal of aircraft after landing was of great importance to the efficiency of the carrier. Up until the early '30s, all aircraft had to be 'struck down' to the hangar on a lift. Even in a ship like the old (1920) HMS *Eagle*, which had a broad forward lift which could accommodate an unfolded aircraft, the lowering and raising cycle alone occupied a minute and time needed for positioning the aircraft on and then manhandling off the lift platform would double that portion of the 'dead time' between landings. In the case of aircraft whose wings required to be folded before being struck down, the minimum interval between landings would be of the order of three minutes, so that the recovery of a squadron of 12 aircraft could take half-an-hour.

The United States Navy revolutionised carrier flying potential by the simple expedient of devising a 'safety barrier'. Stretched across the deck about 150ft forward of the foremost arrester wire (usually in the vicinity of the island), the barrier could be lowered to permit aircraft which had landed safely to taxi forward into a deck park; when raised, the barrier protected the deck park from any aircraft which failed to catch an arrester wire. The landing interval was now limited only by the speed with which the first aircraft to land could disengage from the wires and taxi over the lowered barrier, and also by the time needed to reset the arrester wires for the next landing. In practice, the deck could be clear and the wires ready in under a minute and a well-drilled carrier Air Group could turn in remarkable performances: the *average* interval between Seafire landings aboard HMS *Implacable* during July and August 1945 was 43 seconds, but in one recovery 18 pilots brought this down to 32 seconds.

The US Navy introduced barriers in the mid-1930s, followed shortly afterwards by the Imperial Japanese Navy. The Royal Navy was slow to adopt the barrier, and although HMS *Ark Royal* was completed with a system which would stop an 8,000lb aircraft moving at 40 knots in 40ft, it was not until mid-1940 that the ship began to use the barrier for the intended purpose. One reason for the British delay was an insistence on a design which would inflict less damage on the aircraft being restrained: the American barrier was a somewhat savage affair, strung between two light supports which collapsed as soon as the two steel wires of the barrier were engaged. These wires were paid out from deck level, so that the aircraft was usually tipped forward on to its nose by the final deceleration and consequently suffered varying degrees of damage to the engine and forward fuselage. The British barrier which finally emerged was more gentlemanly in its action and quite different in appearance. The supporting stanchions were sturdy erections intended to carry the full load of the deceleration, the barrier wires being paid out from the top of them, so that the retarding force would be exerted *through* the centre of gravity of the aircraft, instead of from below. To spread the impact load on the aircraft, the barrier itself was in the form of a net, instead of the two simple wires of the American design. The major shortcomings of the British barrier lay in the very sturdiness of the stanchions – an off-centre engagement would result in severe damage to any aircraft striking the supports.

Once safely aboard, aircraft in the deck park forward could be refuelled from the fuel main which ran around the outside of the deck edge, supplying fuel under pressure direct from the bulk fuel tanks. Electrical power points were also provided around the deck edge to eliminate the need for accumulator trolleys in an already overcrowded area. Bomb and torpedo lifts also opened on to the flight deck, so that the entire turn-round routine could be performed without the need to return the aircraft to the hangar.

The main aircraft lift platforms formed part of the load-bearing structure of the flight deck, the after lift being in the landing area in most carriers. The lift machinery installed was usually designed to cope with the intended weights of the aircraft to be operated from the ship, plus a generous allowance. Thus the first carrier of all, HMS *Argus,* was equipped with lifts which could raise or lower 9,000lb (4-ton) aircraft at a time when she was built to operate 4,000lb aircraft. By 1941, most new carriers were being fitted with 16,000lb lifts, operated electrically in British and Japanese ships and hydraulically in American carriers.

The number and size of lifts varied considerably. The Royal Navy's motley collection of early carriers had all been equipped with a T-shaped lift forward which could accommodate a non-folding aircraft. Those ships which boasted a second lift were provided with a large rectangular platform aft, long enough to take a floatplane. The later British armoured carriers were built with two lifts in order that the flight deck protection should not be weakened by too many apertures; for the same reason the lifts were again only 22ft wide in the first three ships, although the last three were given a wider forward lift while under construction.

The US Navy had no cause for concern over the possible weakness involved in having too many large apertures in the flight deck as this deck made no contribution to the strength of the ships which came after USS *Lexington* and *Saratoga.* Three of the next five ships had three large inboard lifts connecting the flight deck and the single hangar. The centre lift was inconvenient, however, for when it was at flight deck level, the hangar was divided by the empty lift well (or 'elevator pit'), and so in the next original design, USS *Essex,* the amidships lift was moved to the port side of the hangar, with its platform projecting outboard beyond the hangar and flight decks. So successful was this repositioning that the deck-edge elevator became standard in the large carriers (CVs) of the 'Essex' and 'Midway' classes and in the post-war 'Forrestal' class all four lifts were around the deck edges.

Japanese ship design was empirical to an extreme. The small *Hosho* had two lifts, but *Kaga* and *Akagi* were equipped with three each – setting the standard for later big carriers. While the apertures were acceptable in ships in which the flight deck and upper hangar deck were not contributing to the longitudinal girder strength, they were a positive weakness in the lightly-built *Hiryu* and *Soryu* and only slightly less surprising to Western designers in the succeeding 'Shokaku' class. It was significant that when a modified *Hiryu* design was ordered one of the major alterations to the layout was the reduction in the number of lifts to two. *Taiho,* the only armoured carrier built in Japan, also had only two lifts but their area was double that of the British 'Illustrious' class. The size of Japanese lift platforms was dictated by aircraft design – fighters and dive-bombers had folding wing-tips only – and the smallest lift in a ship built or converted after 1935 measured 38 × 35½ft (12 × 10.8m).

The modest wing-folding ability of Japanese aircraft was in its turn dictated by the height of the hangars, generally between 13 and 14ft, but in the 'Junyo' class barely 11ft in the lower hangar. British carrier hangars had a standard unobstructed height of 16ft after 1924, until the later armoured carriers had a lower hangar incorporated at a late stage in the design: rather than raise the heavy armoured flight deck and hangar sides by 16ft, the hangar heights were reduced to 14ft each, thus saving 2ft and maintaining ship stability near its previous figure. With the unarmoured 1942 Light Fleet carriers, the Royal Navy was able to increase hangar height to 17½ft – standard in American carriers since the pre-war 'Yorktown' class.

The hangar was a workshop area as well as a protected stowage for aircraft, with overhead lifting gear for the handling of major assemblies such as aero-engines. The larger spare items, such as engines, propellers, mainplanes and tailplanes were stowed around the hangar walls and also in the 'deep beam stowages' up in the hangar deck-heads, between the deep girders which supported the weight of the flight deck. In American ships, considerable lengths of the hangar walls consisted of light steel shutters which could be raised to open the hangar deck to the elements, allowing aircraft engines to be test-run without a build-up of carbon monoxide exhaust fumes in an enclosed space and without interfering with flying operations on the flight deck. When closed, the shutters could not be

Vought Corsairs in ILLUSTRIOUS' *hangar in 1944. The wingtips of the aircraft supplied to the Royal Navy had to be squared off to permit the wings to be folded in the 16-feet high hangars of this class of ship.* (IWM)

relied upon to keep the weather out or to remain light tight – a vital consideration in a darkened ship in wartime. In contrast, British design policy called for a completely closed hangar, access from the remainder of the ship being through double-doored lobbies (the first unforgivable crime was to have both doors of a lobby open at one time), with workshops around the hangar opening only into the hangar; nowhere was the hangar wall also the side of the ship. The Japanese Navy had no such rules and although hangars were enclosed, they were not flash-tight or, as important, vapour-tight.

British precautions were based upon a healthy respect for the explosive qualities of aviation gasoline (AvGas) when its vapour was allowed to spread unchecked. Bulk fuel was stowed in coffer dams surrounded by sea water which provided the pressure to force the AvGas into the fuel mains and prevented a vapour-laden void from forming under the lighter fuel as the fuel was used. The coffer dams were not integral with the hull structure so that vibration of 'whip' caused by bomb hits or near-misses or torpedo hits would not fracture the fuel stowage. The penalties paid for this elaborate system were occasional fuel contamination and a greatly reduced capacity, but no British-built carrier suffered damage from a bulk fuel installation fire or explosion. Japanese and American carriers did not use the water displacement method, preferring to depend upon pumps to provide all pressure in the AvGas mains. In Japanese ships, the tanks formed part of the structure of the hull and were surrounded by an air space filled with inert carbon dioxide gas to prevent an explosive vapour from forming in the event of fractures in the main tank. In an emergency, or when expecting an attack, all the fuel in the supply lines and mains could be drained back down to the tanks and the lines and the void at the top of the tank filled with carbon dioxide.

Careful attention to ventilation arrangements, ensuring that AvGas vapour was exhausted from the hangar to the open air and not allowed to permeate the ship, was also essential to carrier design. The heavy vapour tended to form a layer which seldom rose more than 6ft above the hangar deck level, making it easier to provide low-level exhaust outlets which could renew the air in the hangar every ten minutes. In British and American carriers the fresh air was supplied naturally, through the unavoidable gaps between the lift platform and the flight deck; in the open hangar ships, forced ventilation – intake or exhaust – was unnecessary in normal conditions. The Japanese used intake and exhaust fan systems, which led to circulation of vapour above the normal level – a dangerous condition which was not realised and corrected until after the beginning of the War. Electrical appliances and lighting were obviously essential, but the danger of sparking was minimised by the use of heavy insulation and the positioning of switch gear above the 8-ft level, where the risk of a spark igniting vapour was slight.

It was realised that fires would break out in hangars in spite of all precautions. The first priority in such an event was to prevent it from spreading and once this had been achieved, to get on with fighting the blaze. The three major navies agreed on the best means of containment and by 1930, all had fitted roller-blind-type fire curtains in the hangars of their carriers, the purpose of the steel or fire-proofed fabric curtains being to restrict the supply of air to the fire, as well as to prevent it spreading. The means of fighting the fire were not agreed: the Japanese employed a foam spray system, two rows of pipes and nozzles being fitted to the walls and ends of the hangars, operated from fire-proof lobbies. In addition, a carbon dioxide 'flooding' system was employed on lower hangar decks, where the vapour build-up was likely to be greater. The US Navy employed an overhead spray system to produce a 'water fog' which would extinguish the fire and provide rapid cooling to prevent the fire breaking out again. The fog and curtain system was not as effective as the system employed in British ships, as the open hangar sides permitted the entry of air and the result was that fires had to be fought with hoses as well as the sprays on several occasions. In the British carriers, the combination of a sealed hangar and a high pressure sea-water spray system, fitted since 1930, was highly effective, and the hangar fires which occurred during the War were dealt with in minutes, except when battle damage had wrecked the fire curtains and the spray supply pipes. The disadvantage of the use of sprays in an enclosed hangar was that rapid-flow drains were needed to get rid of the water which would otherwise remain to create a serious danger to ship stability (the second unforgivable crime was to leave any material which might block the scuppers lying around in the hangar). Another problem was that aircraft caught by the spray could suffer write-off damage through salt-water corrosion of alloy parts and the electrical wiring.

Apart from fire precautions, the Japanese and American designers took few steps to enable the hangars to stand up to attack. The hangar floors were armoured to protect the ships' propulsion machinery and magazines, but there was no other protection, except in the Japanese *Taiho* and *Shinano,* which both boasted armoured decks. A bomb detonating in a US Navy carrier's hangar tended to vent the blast through the hangar side openings and the lift openings (when the lifts were lowered). Explosions in Japanese carriers were invariably spectacular in their effects: the blast was contained initially by the closed hangar but as the pressure built up large areas of the structure were distorted, the flight deck being bulged upwards or blown out completely, and similar damage occurring in the weak spots in the hangar walls. The British armoured carriers, with thick walls, ends, roofs and floors for their hangars, could contain the blast of a 1,100lb (500kg) armour-piercing bomb, although the damage to fittings was devastating; in the event, only one armoured carrier took such a heavy bomb in the hangar, the others defeating attacks on their flight deck armour.

Accommodation in carriers was generally poor, there being little room left after the hangar, powerful propulsion machinery and all the necessary fuel, ordnance and spares stowages had been worked in. Mess-decks were fitted in wherever there was sufficient space but as the war progressed the fitting of extra armament and electronics and the carriage of extra aircraft, all requiring more users and maintainers, led to serious overcrowding throughout the ship and to severe strain on the domestic arrangements such as meal times, recreation and washing facilities. By 1945, conditions in a Royal Navy carrier were as uneviable as those aboard a two-decker in Nelson's day.

The location of equipment which had to be mounted on the topsides of ships was always seriously inhibited by the paramount need to leave the flight deck clear. The dual-purpose AA/surface defence guns of between 4-in (100mm) and 5-in (127mm) calibre had to be mounted around the deck edges, experience dictating that they should be below flight deck level to minimise the effects of muzzle blast on parked aircraft. Only the US Navy mounted heavy AA guns above the flight deck, the 'Essex' class featuring twin mountings fore and aft of the island. Light automatic AA guns were fitted wherever they would go, around the deck edges, on the island and, in the case of British ships, on the flight deck fore and aft of the island. Room had also to be found for the fire control directors as close as possible to the batteries which they controlled and the Royal Navy went as far as installing the port-side directors on hydraulically-operated mountings which were lowered to below deck level normally and raised when in action.

Radar aerials presented the greatest problem, however. Sets were required for surface warning and navigation and also for air warning and control, but their necessarily large antennae had to compete with homing beacons, communications aerials and gunnery equipment for the limited number of locations around the island masts. Early British air warning radars required separate transmitting and receiving aerials, so that an additional mast had to be erected; this was retained when a combined aerial was developed and a second set installed to improve the radar coverage. American carriers of the 'Essex' class were fitted with a masthead warning set and the main control radar was installed on a bracket projecting to starboard of the island. The Japanese did not possess an operational shipborne radar until 1942, but their islands were generally smaller than those in the Western carriers and the main radar was therefore mounted on top of a pill-box on the flight deck, port side aft, a position where it was well clear of funnel gases and imposed less of a stability problem.

Fitted in wherever possible were the various communications aerials – High Frequency sets for inter-ship and ship-air use requiring wire aerials strung between the 'hockey post' masts located along the flight deck sides, and, from 1942, Very High Frequency sets for short-range inter-ship, and all air communications. The location of the small 'blade' or 'whip' aerials of the latter was critical as there was liable to be very heavy mutual interference between the sets if they were too close together and yet the short permissible length of the leads between the sets and the aerials meant that the latter had to be situated in a group. For this reason, few carriers could fit more than five VHF aerials although as many as ten VHF sets might be carried.

The demands of all the electronics in addition to the lighting and machinery requirements called for a very considerable electrical generating capacity. Whereas in 1935 all demands could be met by the provision of turbo-generators with a total output of less than 2,500kW, by 1943 it was obvious that over 3,000kW was required aboard the same ship, the additional power being supplied by diesel generators which continued to function although steam might not be available for the turbo-generators through action damage. The loss of HMS *Ark Royal* through slow flooding when pumping power was lost with the extinguishing of the last of her boilers, served to underline the necessity for diesel generators independent of the main machinery.

The need to incorporate the special features for aviation purposes as well as the conventional ship's services thus presented the designers with special problems which became ever greater. No set pattern for carrier design could be laid down and thereafter followed, for development of ancillary equipment resulted in continuing changes in the requirements – the only constant being the need for a flat 'roof' over a box for holding aircraft.

France

Béarn

The only French carrier to be completed before 1960, *Béarn* was originally laid down in 1914 as a 'Normandie' class dreadnought battleship. Construction was suspended during the First World War but resumed in 1919, the ship being launched in April 1920. Landing-on trials were conducted in 1920 and 1921 with a short flight deck erected over the quarterdeck and in April 1922, two months after the Washington Treaty had been signed, it was decided to complete *Béarn* as a carrier. The Treaty signatories had agreed that only those ships begun or complete at the time of signature should be considered exempt from the total national tonnage allowance, but the French managed to obtain an exemption on the grounds that *Béarn* had already been used for flying trials. Work actually began on the conversion in August 1923. Assistance was provided by the British Admiralty, in the form of the drawings of HMS *Eagle's* aviation and island arrangements. Lack of money delayed completion until May 1927 and thereafter had a serious effect on the provision of aircraft, to the extent that in September 1939 she was carrying a handful of 1931-vintage Levasseur torpedo-bombers and fewer than 20 unreliable Dewoitine D37-series fighters. The aircraft were withdrawn from front-line service by the end of November 1939 and *Béarn* thereafter served as an aircraft transport between France and the USA; she was at Martinique when the Armistice was signed in June 1940 and lay there inactive for three years, until the island changed its allegiance from Vichy to the Free French Government. After a refit in the USA she resumed aircraft transport duties for the remainder of the War and for some while thereafter. After serving as an accommodation ship the *Béarn* was scrapped in 1967-68.

Hull: The hangars and flight deck were built on the original fo'c'sle deck, and the ship's side aft plated up to fo'c'sle deck level. Waterline belt armour was reduced to 3.15in (80mm) from 9.5in, lower hangar deck 2.95in (75mm), main deck 1in (25mm).

Flight Deck and Hangars: The 1in armour flight deck, extending the full length of the ship, with pronounced round-downs fore and aft, was supported by pillars and webs and constituted the upper strength girder of the ship. Connected to two hangars by three electrically-operated lifts which were unique in that the platforms did not form part of the flight deck area but were normally maintained at upper hangar deck level, the apertures in the flight deck being closed by 'clam-shell' doors which served as wind-breaks when opened with the lift platform at flight deck level. The upper hangar was used to stow operational aircraft and the lower was a workshop and reserve aircraft stowage area. Aircraft capacity was officially stated as being 40 of all types, but this number included the reserve and the maximum number which could be operated did not exceed 25. Transverse arrester wires, electrically controlled, were installed from 1927, the maximum permissible aircraft weight being 4,000kg (8,800lb) following modernisation in 1935.

Machinery: The main propulsion machinery was also unique, for the two inner shafts were driven by steam turbines while the two outer shafts were driven by steam reciprocating engines, in an attempt

BÉARN *was fitted with a huge trapeze-like 'spreader' on the funnel for rigging W/T aerials instead of the more usual deck-edge 'hockey sticks'. Unlike HMS* EAGLE *her original battleship fo'c'sle was not plated up to fair with of the flight deck.*

to combine the economy of the latter with the high speed performance of the former. Unfortunately, the standards aimed at were those of 1914 rather than 1927 and by 1939 her maximum speed of 21 knots was too low for effective operation with the 29-knot battleships of the *Force de Raid,* while her best radius of action was achieved at 10 knots. After two months spent hunting for German surface raiders and blockade runners *Béarn* was withdrawn from operations, her activities having been severely circumscribed by her low speed and the unreliability of her few aircraft.

Armament: The gun armament was conventional for the period, consisting of eight 155mm guns mounted in 70mm (2¾in) armoured casemates, for use against destroyers and light craft. Six 75mm AA guns were mounted in sponsons on the sides of the ship below flight deck level; eight 37mm automatic AA guns were added, apparently at the time of a major refit in 1935. *Béarn* was the only post-1918 aircraft carrier to be armed with torpedo-tubes, possessing four underwater tubes; the circumstances under which these could have been used can only be described as dire, for their maximum slow-speed range was 20,000m (22,000yds) – less than the range of the guns of capital ships and heavy cruisers which would be the only targets worthy of the torpedoes.

Béarn

Displacement tonnage	
Standard	22,146
Full load	28,400
Dimensions	
Length (oa)	599ft 1in (182.6m)
Beam (wl)	88ft 11in (27.1m) 115ft 6in (35.2m) max
Draught (mean)	30ft 6in (9.3m)
Flight deck	590ft 6in (180m) × 88ft 7in (27m)
Hangars (upper)	406ft 10in (124m) × 64ft (19.5m)
(lower)	321ft 6in (98m) × 59ft (18m)
Lifts	3 – largest 50ft × 51.5ft (15.25m × 15.7m)
Aircraft stowage	40 (including reserves)
Machinery	2 sets turbines, 2 sets triple expansion; 4 shafts
total hp	37,200 (15,000 ihp + 22,200 shp)
speed	21.5 knots (trials)
fuel	2,037 tons
radius	6,000nm (6,910 statute miles = 11,050km) at 10 knots; 4,500nm at 18 knots
Armament	8 × 155mm (6.1-in) in armoured casemates 6 × 75mm (2.95-in) AA 8 × 37mm AA 4 × 550mm (21.65-in) TT
Complement	875
Builder	Chantiers de la Méditerranée, La Seyne, Toulon
Launched	April 1920 (as battleship)
Completed	May 1927

Germany

Graf Zeppelin

Design work on Germany's first aircraft carrier was initiated in the spring of 1934, when the most advanced carrier in service with a European Navy was HMS *Glorious,* completed four years earlier. In 1935, Germany entered into a Naval Treaty with Britain after repudiating the terms of the Versailles Treaty which had, among other restrictions, forbidden the formation of a naval air force. Under the terms of the 1935 London Treaty, Germany was allowed to build carriers up to a total tonnage of 47,250 (standard), individual ships being limited to 23,000 tons. Germany decided to build two 23,430-ton ships; the marginal excess was pardonable, the declaration that their standard displacement was to be 19,250 tons was not.

Flugzeugträger A was laid down in mid-1937 and launched at the end of 1938, by which time *"B"* had also been laid down. Work on the first, named *Graf Zeppelin,* was suspended in April 1940, when she was 90% complete but was experiencing difficulties with the development and fitting of the arrester gear and catapults. These problems had still not been resolved when work was resumed for seven months in 1942/3. Construction was halted for all time in February 1943 and she was laid up until scuttled at Stettin on 24 April 1945. Raised by the Soviets, she was loaded with war booty and towed to Leningrad, striking mines in the Gulf of Finland and the approaches to Leningrad. *Graf Zeppelin* was scrapped in 1948. *Flugzeugträger B* was dismantled in 1940, having been completed only as far as the armoured deck when the first carrier suspension order had been given.

Hull: *Graf Zeppelin* had the greatest beam of any carrier designed before 1942, thanks to the addition of deep bulges to improve stability and underwater defence and also to reduce the draught. With a waterline length:breadth ratio of 8.33:1 she needed very powerful machinery to reach her designed speed. The flight deck was the upper strength deck but was lightly protected, with a thickness of only 20mm over the hangar. Indeed, the scale of protection was light throughout the ship, with only 60mm (2.36in) over the magazines and 40mm over the machinery, set in one deck just above the waterline. The belt was 100mm (3.9in) thick abreast the machinery and 60mm fore and aft, backed by an internal anti-torpedo splinter bulkhead 20mm thick.

Flight Deck and Hangar: The original design incorporated a flying-off deck ahead of the lower

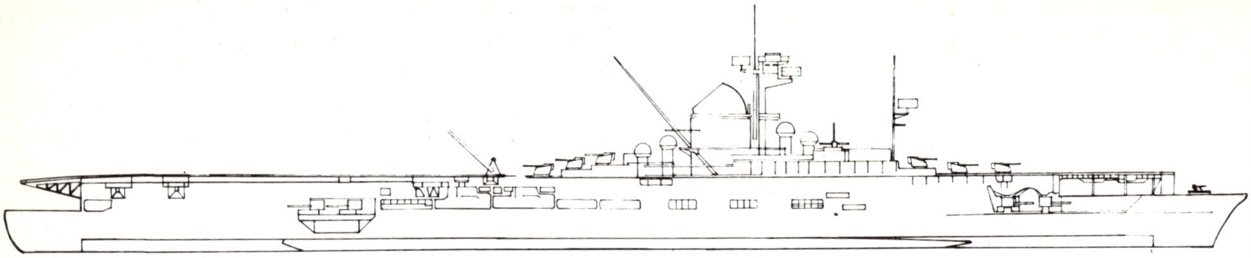

GRAF ZEPPELIN: *1942 design*

hangar (as in HMS *Glorious)* but by the time that the ship was laid down it was obvious that some form of assistance would be needed to launch aircraft at high all-up-weights and two Deutsche Werke catapults were to be fitted flush with the flight deck, right forward. The trolleys from which the aircraft were launched could be loaded in the hangars and transferred to the "accelerators" by means of a 'railway system' which extended aft to the amidships lift. Three lifts were provided to connect the flight deck with the two large hangars, the size and number of lifts seeming to be rather excessive for a ship intended to operate only 42 aircraft. The hangars were extremely long but rather narrow, the Germans having followed British practice in providing workshops, stores and accommodation outboard of the hangar. Total hangar area was greater than that in the 1934-designed HMS *Ark Royal,* with a complement of 18 fewer aircraft. Considerable attention had been paid to the aerodynamics of the flight deck and superstructure, airflow patterns being investigated in a wind tunnel. The open fo'c'sle and uneven flight deck leading edge did not appear to cause much turbulence, but the long low island did generate a vortex over the landing area when the ship yawed to port; the after end of the flight deck was slightly rounded-down, though not as much as in British ships.

Machinery: The four-shaft geared turbine machinery was the most powerful yet designed for a warship and was not exceeded until the appearance of the American 'Iowa' class battleships in 1943. The effect of the broad beam is evident when the intended 33.8 knots at 28,000 tons is compared with the achievement of the Japanese *Shokaku,* which was half a knot faster at 29,800 tons with 20% less power!

Armament: The primary armament consisted of 16 150mm (5.9in) low-angle guns mounted in pairs in casemates, distributed at the 'corners' of the upper hangar deck; such guns were rather limited in their application and the other navies were fitting dual-purpose anti-aircraft/anti-shipping guns at this time. Twelve 105mm (4.1-in) AA guns were installed in six twin mountings, three ahead of and three abaft the island. Although such an arrangement simplified fire control, with four stabilised directors located in the inordinately long island, gun blast would have limited flight deck activity. Close-range armament consisted of 11 twin-37mm and seven single 20mm guns around the deck edges and fore and aft.

Graf Zeppelin

Note: Data official estimates where applicable

Displacement tonnage	
Standard	19,250 (declared)
	23,430 (actual planned)
Full load	33,550 (1942 Revision)
Dimensions	
Length (oa)	861ft 3in (262.5m)
Beam (wl)	103ft 4in (31.5m)
(max)	118ft 9in (36.2m)
Draught	27ft 108in (8.5m)
Flight deck	787ft 5in (240m) × 88ft 7in (27m)
Hangars (upper)	600ft 5in (183m) × 52ft 6in (16m)
(lower)	557ft 9in (170m) × 52ft 6in
Lifts	3 – all approx 50ft (15.2m) × 47ft (14.3m)
Catapults	2: 11,000lb (5,000kg) @ 72kts (83mph = 133kph)
Aircraft stowage	42
Machinery	4 sets geared turbines; 4 shafts
shp	200,000 (designed)
speed	33.8 knots (at 27,650 tons)
fuel	6,156 tons
radius	8000nm (9,200 stm = 14,740km) at 18 knots
Armament	16 × 150mm (5.9-in) in casemates
	6 × 2 105mm (4.1-in) AA in open mountings
	11 × 2 37mm AA
	28 × 20mm (single and quadruple mountings)
Complement	1,760 (not including aviation personnel)
Builder	Deutsche Werke, Kiel
Launched	8 December 1938
Completed	92% in 1942

Italy

Aquila

The Italian Naval Staff ordered the design of an aircraft carrier in 1932 but this ship did not proceed beyond the drawing board; certain features were, however, revived in June 1940, following Italy's entry into the War, when it was planned to convert the 38,000-ton 21-knot Transatlantic liner *Roma* into an auxiliary carrier. Authority for a rapid, simple conversion, with a flush deck and small hangar was given at the end of 1940, but on 27 January 1941 the order was rescinded, following the damage inflicted on HMS *Illustrious* by German dive-bombers. A further study was ordered in July 1941 and *Roma,* re-named *Aquila* (Eagle), was taken in hand at Genoa in November. The conversion was the most comprehensive ever attempted, the Japanese 'Junyo' class not excepted, and had she been completed in time to see service then she could have proved to be a formidable opponent.

Hull: The liner's interior was virtually gutted to replace the machinery and build in a hangar and workships. The bows were lengthened to improve the lines forward to take full advantage of the extra power and the deep bulges which were added amidships from above the waterline to below the original bottom also contributed to the finer lines, as well as maintaining stability and providing some anti-torpedo defence. The only other protection consisted of a layer of concrete, 60 to 80mm (2.4 to 3.1in) thick inboard of the bulge, and 30 to 80mm of armour over the magazines and aviation fuel stowages. The latter followed British practice, taking the form of cylindrical tanks separate from the structure of the ship, in water-filled compartments. Lacking major armour protection, the Italians opted for extensive internal sub-division, backed by adequate pump capacity, to contain and correct flooding.

Flight Deck and Hangar: The flight deck ended short of the bows but overhung the stern, with a distinct round-down to improve the airflow. Two Heinkel catapults (accelerators) were installed right forward, as in *Graf Zeppelin,* and a similar trolley 'railway system' extended aft to the lifts and thence into the hangar. The position of the lifts was unusual, abreast the fore and aft ends of the island, but the platforms were thus well clear of the four widely-spaced arrester wires and could both be used for striking-down aircraft immediately after landing. The octagonal lift-wells, 50 ft wide, divided the hangar into three bays, but the loss of stowage area was overcome by the ingenious method of slinging complete aircraft from the roof of the hangar. In this way, 41 non-folding Reggiane Re 2001 fighter-bombers could be accommodated in the hangar, 15 hanging from the deck-head. Another ten Re 2001s were to have been kept on deck in a permanent deck park, giving *Aquila* a very respectable aircraft complement.

Machinery: The liner's 38,500hp turbines were replaced by four sets of geared turbines originally ordered for two light cruisers of the 'Capitani Romani' class. With over 150,000hp now available, it was believed that the ship would reach 30 knots on trials and have a sea speed of 29.5 knots fully laden.

Armament: The Italians lacked a heavy dual-purpose weapon, but the eight 135mm (5.4-in) guns, taken from a cancelled 'Capitani Romani', had an elevation of 45° and could be usefully employed for barrage fire. The main AA armament consisted of six 65mm guns on either side of the hull, mounted below the flight deck. Sixteen 6-barrelled 20mm AA guns were also mounted below flight deck level, as well as six mountings on the island. The 135mm fire control directors were mounted on a tall 'tower' above the bridge on the island, which otherwise bore a closer resemblance to those in Allied ships, being shorter and taller than that in *Graf Zeppelin.*

Fate: *Aquila* was practically ready for sea trials when the Italian Government concluded an armistice with the Allies on 8 September 1943, but was sabotaged by her own crew on the following day in order to prevent the Germans from completing her. She was scuttled by the Germans to block part of

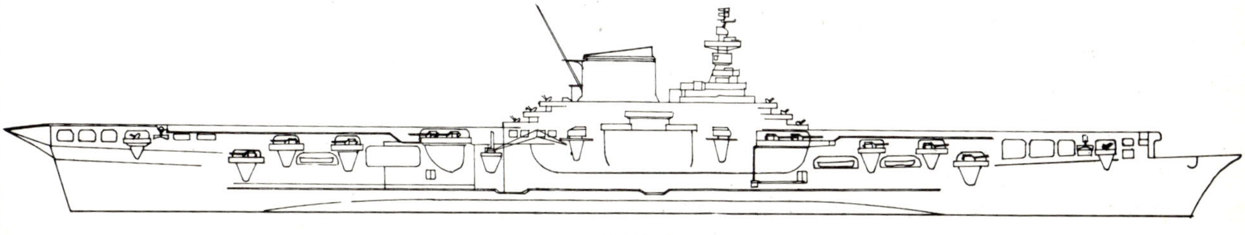

AQUILA: *1943 design*

Genoa harbour in April 1945. Raised in 1946, she was then towed to La Spezia in 1949 and after consideration had been given to completing her or converting her to some other use, *Aquila* was finally broken up in 1952.

Aquila

Note: Data official estimates where applicable

Displacement tonnage	
Standard	23,500
Full load (normal)	27,800
Full load (max)	28,800
Dimensions	
Length (oa)	759ft 2in (211.6m)
Beam (wl)	98ft 7in (30m)
Draught	24ft 3in (7.4m) at 27,800 tons
Flight deck	694ft 3in (211.6m) × 82ft 8in (25.2m)
Hangar	524ft 11in × 59ft (160m × 18m)
Lifts	2 – 50ft × 50ft (15.2m × 15.2m) (max)
Arrester wires	4
Catapults	2 – as *Graf Zeppelin*
Aircraft stowage	51
Machinery	4 sets geared turbines; 4 shafts
shp	151,000
speed	30 knots
fuel	2,800 tons (normal), 3,660 tons (max)
radius (normal)	4,150 nm (4,780 stm = 7,650km) at 18 knots
(max)	5,500nm (6,330 stm = 10,300km) at 18 knots
Armament	8 × 5.3-in (135mm) low angle
	12 × 2.56-in (65mm) AA
	22 × 6 20mm AA
Complement	1,420
Conversion	Ansaldo, Genoa: July 1941-8 September 1943 (sabotaged before completion)

Japan

Hosho

The first Japanese carrier, *Hosho* (Swooping Dragon), was laid down as an oiler in 1919. Building was suspended in 1920, after the Imperial Japanese Navy decided to complete her as a carrier, until the revised design could be worked out (with the aid of the British Technical Mission which had arrived in Japan at the invitation of the Japanese Navy to assist in building up a modern naval air force). After launching in November 1921, *Hosho* was towed to the Yokosuka Navy Yard for fitting out and was commissioned on 27 December 1922, the first deck-landing being achieved in late February, 1923.

Hull: The original tanker hull was modified but little, apart from the re-routing of the funnel uptakes and the internal stowage and accommodation arrangements. The hangar was on the original tank deck which, because it had neither camber nor sheer, was ideal for handling and aircraft stowage. The extra topweight of the flight deck was compensated by a Sperry stabilisation system which worked well in *Hosho's* 59-ft wide hull but which encouraged the Japanese to take undue liberties in a later ship.

Flight Deck and Hangar: *Hosho's* flight deck extended for the full length of the ship, supported by the hangar walls and pillars fore and aft. Made of steel, its factor of strength was intended to be twice the landing energy of the heaviest aircraft to be embarked, an arbitrary figure selected and retained by the Japanese for most of their carrier designs. In *Hosho's* case, this was based on a maximum aircraft weight of 8,800lb (4,000kg), but it was later increased to 13,200lb (6,000kg); arrester gear and lifts were designed to operate to the same loads.

The hangar was a box-like structure, the forward section being about 40ft wide and the after third extending the full beam of the ship. A short length of the hangar sides amidships was open, but this was found to be unsatisfactory as in heavy weather seas tended to enter the hangar – only about 15ft above the waterline – and at night the shutters covering the apertures showed light around their edges; the sides were therefore plated over and the Japanese disregarded the open hangar until 1942. The low narrow hangar had a useful length of about 300ft, restricting aircraft capacity to a maximum of 21 when first commissioned; by 1942, with larger, heavier aircraft, her complement was less than a dozen.

As first completed, *Hosho* sported a small starboard-side island, consisting of little more than

HOSHO *as she appeared when first completed, with a starboard-side island, open hangar amidships and downward-sloping forward flight deck.* (IJN OFFICIAL)

a navigating bridge above a chart-house. This was disliked by the trials pilots, landing on such a narrow flight deck, and it was removed immediately after the trials; the navigating position was removed to wing platforms on either side of the forward end of the hangar box, the chart-house looking forward between the pillars supporting the forward overhang of the flight deck.

At some stage, *Hosho* was fitted with a system of approach lights to assist pilots with the right angle of approach to the deck. This appears to have resembled the Airfield Approach Light and Royal Navy's 'Sector Lights' systems, using a triple red-amber-green light projector to enable the pilot to see for himself whether he was low, correct, or high on his approach. Although the system was not as accurate as post-War optical deck-landing aids, nor could it be stabilised to eliminate the effects of the ship pitching, the Japanese were sufficiently satisfied for it to become the standard system for later carriers and for them never to feel the need of a 'batsman'.

Machinery: The original reciprocating machinery was replaced by two sets of destroyer-type geared turbines, steam being provided by twelve boilers in six boiler rooms. The uptakes from the boilers were carried across to the starboard side to exhaust through three stacks amidships, hinged to move between a horizontal position during flying operations and the vertical when cruising; such an arrangement had been discussed in 1918 for HMS *Eagle* and had actually been pioneered in a British tanker, the *War Rambler*.

Armament: As completed, *Hosho* mounted four 140mm (5.51-in) low-angle guns outboard of the hangar and two 76.2mm (3-in) AA guns on the flight deck, to port and starboard. By 1942, all these guns had been removed and the armament consisted of eight twin 25mm automatic AA guns (French Hotchkiss guns built under licence as the Type 96).

Fate: *Hosho* was employed as a deck-landing training ship for most of the War, taking part only in the Midway operation. She was scrapped at Osaka in 1947 after repatriation transport duties.

Hosho

Displacement tonnage (1923)	
Standard	7,470
Full load	10,000
Dimensions	
Length (oa) 1923	551ft 5in (168.1m)
1944	579ft 5in (176.6m)
Beam (wl)	59ft 1in (18m)
Draught	20ft 3in (6.17m)
Flight deck 1923	519ft (158.2m) × 74ft 6in (22.7m)
1944	547ft (166.7m) × 74ft 6in
Hangar	423ft 6in (129m) × 40-55ft (12.2-16.8m)
Arrester wires	6
Lifts	2 – largest 40ft × 27ft 10in (12.8m × 8.5m)
Aircraft stowage	21, reducing to 11 in 1942
Machinery	2 sets geared turbines; 2 shafts
shp	30,000
speed	25 knots
radius	approx 3,000nm (3,455 st m = 5,525km) at 14 knots
Armament 1923	4 × 140mm (5.51-in) in open shields
	2 × 76.2m (3-in) AA
	2 × 7.7mm AA mgs
1942	8 × 2.25mm AA
Complement	550
Builder	Asano SB Co, Tsurumi
Launched	13 November 1921
Fitted out	Yokosuka Navy Yard
Completed	27 December 1922

Akagi

Following the abandonment of capital ship construction after the signature of the Washington Treaty, the Japanese decided to complete two as yet unlaunched battlecruiser hulls as aircraft carriers. One, *Amagi,* was badly damaged on the slip at Yokosuka by the 1923 earthquake and her place was taken by *Kaga,* described later.

Reconstruction of *Akagi* (Red Castle – an extinct volcano) began on 19 November 1923; she was launched on 22 April 1925 and completed on 25 March 1927 – the seventh 'flat-top' to enter service. In this first form she was truly flat topped, for she had a flush flight deck 632ft long over two hangars. Forward of the two hangars were two flying-off platforms, the 60-ft upper one for fighters and the 160-ft lower platform for heavier aircraft, thus leaving the flight deck free for landings. The uptakes from the 19 boilers were led to an unusual funnel arrangement on the starboard side amidships, one large stack exhausting the smoke downwards and outboard and the other, smaller, stack exhausting upwards, below the flight deck. The heaviest calibre guns permitted by Treaty were installed, with six 203.2m (8-in) guns in casemates aft and four in two turrets, one on either side of the upper flying-off deck. Anti-aircraft armament consisted of 12 × 120mm (4.72-in) guns in twin mountings on sponsons below the flight deck to port and starboard. The gun turrets and casemates were armoured and the waterline belt was adequate, although less than the 254mm (10 in) of the original battlecruiser design. The declared standard tonnage was 26,900 – 100 tons inside the limit – but was in fact over 30,000 tons. Aircraft capacity was 60.

In 1936, *Akagi* was taken in hand for modernisation at the Sasebo Navy Yard, following a similar job on *Kaga.* When she emerged, she was capable of operating up to 72 modern aircraft from a full-length flight deck and much enlarged hangars, as well as significant other alterations.

Hull: The most important change to the hull was the addition of a 4ft wide anti-torpedo bulge on each side, to improve stability as well as to provide a more-up-to-date underwater defence. Otherwise, protection remained as it had been, with no horizontal armour other than a thin armoured deck low down, affording no protection to the hangars or even the poorly-designed (from the point of view of safety) aviation fuel stowage. Sub-division was adequate but damage control equipment and personnel training were not – an all-too-common failing in the Imperial Japanese Navy.

Flight Deck and Hangars: The most obvious difference between the original *Akagi* and the reconstructed ship, apart from the extended deck, was the erection of a diminutive island on the port side, amidships. Not so evident was the lengthening of both hangars by some 80ft, the addition of a third large lift just abaft the island, and the replacement of the six electrically-controlled arrester wires by two much lighter hydraulic units controlling nine wires. No catapult or accelerator was ever fitted in this, or any other, Japanese carrier. The maximum aircraft capacity was 91, but the practical operating figure was 72.

This port-side view of AKAGI *at anchor illustrates the enormous freeboard at the flight deck, supported fore and aft by inclined pillars and, amidships, by the sides of the two hangar decks above the original battlecruiser hull.*
(VIA USNI)

AKAGI *after reconstruction with full-length flight deck and port-side island. The three Mitsubishi 'Zero' fighters are parked forward.*
(VIA USNI)

Machinery: The original alternative coal-oil burning boilers were replaced by oil-only boilers and the output was increased slightly, to 133,000shp, to give a maximum trials speed of 31.2 knots. The two funnels gave way to a single long downward-facing stack, still on the starboard side.
Armament: With the elimination of the two flying-off decks, the two forward turrets were deleted, leaving *Akagi* with just six 203.2mm guns in the virtually unusable casemate positions right aft. The six twin 120mm AA guns were retained – somewhat surprisingly, as by 1938 the twin 127mm (5-in) dual-purpose gun was being fitted to modernised ships. The main improvement was the installation of 28 25mm AA guns around the deck edges.

On re-entering service, *Akagi's* standard displacement was admitted to be 36,500 tons – an increase of nearly 10,000 tons which cannot be explained by the alterations, for no extra armour had been added and two heavy 203.2mm turrets had been removed.
Fate: On 4 June 1942 *Akagi* was hit NW of Midway by one 1,000lb (454kg) and one 500lb (227kg) bomb, dropped by dive-bombers from USS *Enterprise.* The fuelled and armed aircraft on board caught fire and although the ship's ability to steam and stay afloat was not directly impaired at first, the rapid spread of the fires forced the abandonment of the machinery spaces: the consequent loss of power meant that little could be done to bring the fires under control and *Akagi* had to be abandoned and scuttled.

Akagi (1938-42)

Displacement tonnage	
Standard	36,500
Full load	42,750
Dimensions	
Length (oa)	855ft 4in (260.7m)
Beam (wl)	102ft 9in (31.32m)
Draught	28ft 7in (8.71m)
Flight deck	817ft 6in (249.17m) × 100ft 1in (30.5m)
Hangars (both)	620ft (188m) × 75ft (22.7m) approx
Arrester wires	9
Lifts	3 – largest 50ft (15.25m) × 39ft 3in (12m)
Aircraft stowage	72 operational
Machinery	4 sets geared turbines; 4 shafts
shp	133,000
speed	31.2 knots
oil fuel	6,000 tons
radius	8,200nm (9,440 stm = 15,100km) at 16 knots
Armament	6 × 203.2m (8-in) in casemates
	6 × 2 120mm (4.72-in) AA
	14 × 2 25mm AA
Complement	2,000
Builder	Kure Navy Yard
Launched	22 April 1925
Completed	25 March 1927
Reconstructed	Sasebo NY (1937-38)
Completed	31 August 1938

Kaga

Laid down as battleship on 19 July 1920 and launched on 17 November 1921, before the signature of the Washington Treaty, *Kaga* (named after a former Japanese province) would have been scrapped had not *Amagi* been damaged in the 1923 earthquake. *Kaga* was substituted and work on the conversion/completion was begun before the end of 1923.
Akagi, but joining the Fleet only in 1930, she resembled the latter in all major respects but one – her funnel arrangements. Whereas *Akagi's* boiler uptakes had been led across to the starboard side to the short midships funnels, *Kaga's* were divided to port and starboard and led aft through trunking running down the outside of the upper hangar deck for a distance of over 300ft to exhaust over the quarterdeck – a system similar to, and as unpopular as, that in HMS *Furious.*

Kaga's battleship hull was some 62ft shorter than *Akagi's* and the flight deck was correspondingly shorter, but the hangars were carried further aft and were slightly wider, so that her aircraft complement was the same. The machinery installation was less powerful and maximum speed was 27.5 knots at a trials displacement of 33,160 tons: assuming that trials were run with two-thirds fuel embarked, then this would indicate a standard displacement of 29,660 tons – well above the 26,000 tons declared by the Imperial Japanese Navy. By 1934 it was evident that the arrangement of flying-off decks had little future, due to the increase in aircraft weights and take-off speeds, and *Kaga* was sent for modernisation at the Sasebo Navy Yard. In her case, the modifications were even more extensive than those to *Akagi* and her usefulness was vastly increased.
Hull: A 34ft section was inserted in the hull abaft the hangar to preserve the length-to-beam ratio after the addition of 9½ft anti-torpedo bulges. The existing 280mm (11in) inclined armour belt remained the principal protection, with a thin armour deck over the magazines but the usual lack of cover for the 600 tons of petrol.
Flight Deck and Hangars: The flight deck was extended to the full length of the lengthened hull (*Akagi's* terminated short of the stem and the stern), carried aft by two sets of distinctive V-struts. Nine arrester wires and two safety barriers, all capable of stopping 6,000kg (13,200lb) aircraft were installed, in place of the six 4,000kg electrically-controlled wires. Both hangars were extended forward and a third large lift was added to serve this area. Outboard of the centre lift there appeared the first permanent island to be built on a Japanese carrier, bearing the main surface armament fire-control director above the bridge and aviation control posi-

KAGA *could be distinguished from* AKAGI *by the narrower smoke stack, the flight deck which extended for the full length of the ship and, of course, the starboard-side island.*
(VIA USNI)

tions. This island, on the starboard side, was realised to be essential by the Japanese and all subsequent large carriers were built with islands, although *Akagi* and *Hiryu* were to preserve the Japanese flair for the unorthodox by having theirs located to port.

Like *Akagi, Kaga* had a maximum capacity of 90 aircraft and she actually operated 81; early wartime experience showed that she was overcrowded and after Pearl Harbor the standard complement was reduced to 66.

Machinery: The original turbines and boilers were stripped out and modern high-pressure boilers and geared turbines installed, raising the power from 91,000 to 127,400shp. Thanks to the lengthening of the hull, the maximum speed was increased slightly, in spite of an increase of 8,800 tons in the trials displacement. Concurrent with the replacement of the machinery the boiler uptakes were all routed to the starboard side, to exhaust through a single downward-facing funnel amidships, the long trunked funnels having proved to be thoroughly unsatisfactory.

Armament: The 203.2mm turrets at upper hangar deck level were suppressed and the guns removed to casemates in the batteries aft, barely 15 feet above the waterline, where they would be virtually useless in even a moderate sea. The heavy AA armament was greatly improved, the 12 × 120mm guns giving way to 16 × 127mm (5-in) weapons in twin mountings, four on either side in sponsons fixed just below the level of the flight deck, with each battery controlled by a modern AA director. Twenty-two 25mm AA guns were also installed, but by 1941 eight more twin mountings had been added, to raise the total to 30 barrels.

Fate: *Kaga* was sunk at Midway on 4 June 1942, four 1,000lb bombs dropped by USS *Enterprise's* dive-bombers reducing her unprotected flight and hangar decks to a blazing shambles. Abandoned soon after the attack, she blew up nine hours later when the fires reached her aviation fuel tanks.

KAGA *was completed in 1928 but was not operational until 1930. The large 8-in turrets can be seen on either side of the upper flying-off deck. Note that the forward lift is offset to starboard.*

Kaga (1936-42)

Displacement tonnage	
Standard	38,200
Full load	43,650
Dimensions	
Length (oa)	815ft 6in (248.58m)
Beam (wl)	106ft 7in (32.5m)
Draught	31ft 1in (9.5m)
Flight deck	815ft 6in × 100ft (30.5m)
Hangars (both)	615ft (187.25m) × 88ft (26.8m) approx
Arrester wires	9
Lifts	3 – largest 48ft 4in (14.75m) × 34ft 3in (10.5m)
Aircraft stowage	81 reducing to 66
Machinery	4 sets geared turbines; 4 shafts
shp	127,400
speed	28.34 knots
oil fuel	5,300 tons
radius	10,000nm (11,500 stm = 18,425km) at 16 kts)
Armament	10 × 203,2mm (8-in) in casemates 8 × 2 127mm (5-in) DP 15 × 2 25mm AA
Complement	2,016
Builder	Kawasaki Dy Co, Kobe
Launched	17 November 1921 (as battleship)
Completed	31 March 1928
Reconstructed	Sasebo NY (1934-35)
Completed	25 June 1935

Ryujo

With the completion of *Kaga* and *Akagi,* the Japanese had used up nearly 53,000 of their total allocation of 83,000 tons for carrier construction. If the Fleet was to have sufficient ships, then lighter carriers would have to be built, but at the same time they would have to be big enough to carry a worthwhile number of aircraft and fast enough to operate with the Fleet. Almost incredibly, the Japanese managed to reconcile these contradictory requirements in a 29-knot 590ft long carrier with stowage for 48 aircraft and a displacement of only 8,000 tons. *Ryujo* (Prancing Dragon), the first Japanese essay at an *ab initio* carrier design was approved in 1927, laid down in 1929 and completed on 9 May 1933.

Hull: The need to keep the weight down resulted in the basic hull being given a very low profile, freeboard amidships being barely 15ft, reducing to 10ft right aft. The fore and aft girder strength was less than was desirable, but the worst feature was the stability. *Ryujo* had originally been designed as a single-hangar ship, but between the ordering and laying down a doubled aircraft complement was demanded, the only possible answer being to superimpose an additional hangar. The total freeboard was thereby increased to 49ft on a beam of 67ft, with a draught of 18ft. Sperry active stabilisers were fitted but these proved quite unable to compensate for the basic instability of the ship – a common fault in Japanese ships designed to stretch the Treaty limits. After a year in service, *Ryujo* went to a Navy Yard for modifications which included the strengthening of the keel and the fitting of enlarged bulges and the removal of two twin 127mm gun mountings. Stability was thereby much improved and a later modification – the raising of the fo'c'sle by nearly ten feet – reduced the tendency to dig the bows in heavy seas. No armour could be worked in because of the weight limitations, but protective plating was incorporated on the sides, outboard of the machinery and magazine spaces.

Flight Deck and Hangars: The flush flight deck formed a 'lid' for the vast 'box' of the hangars, which began 77ft abaft the stem. The navigating bridge occupied a 'glass-house' under the forward lip of the flight deck. Six arrester wires were installed, these being modernised in 1936 to take 6,000kg aircraft. Two lifts connected the flight deck with both hangars, but while the forward platform was large, the after one was diminutive, measuring just 35ft × 23ft, and by 1940 was incapable of accommodating any aircraft in front-line service, except possibly the Nakajima B5N 'Kate' torpedo-bomber (and then only if spotted at an angle). *Ryujo* was therefore virtually a single-lift carrier – a serious limitation in view of her intended aircraft complement. As in the larger ships, the maximum number of aircraft which could be operated was less than the maximum stowage – 37 instead of 48.

A poor-quality photograph of RYUJO *seen operating Nakajima 'Kate' torpedo-bombers. A maximum of six of these 51-feet span aircraft could be ranged for take-off from this ship's short, 75-feet wide deck.* (SHIPS OF THE WORLD)

RYUJO *was completed with three twin 5-in guns on each side but these were removed in 1934 to improve stability. Here she is seen at full speed during her initial trials in 1933.* (SHIPS OF THE WORLD)

Machinery: The machinery installation was essentially two units of the type installed in the 'Takao' class heavy cruisers, giving a maximum speed of 29 knots on trials. The boiler uptakes were led to the starboard side, where they exhausted through two relatively small curved funnels which were supported at their outboard ends, roughly level with the upper hangar, by lattice bracing.
Armament: When completed, *Ryujo* carried three twin 127mm dual-purpose guns on sponsons on each side of the hull. The 1934 reductions in topweight involved the sacrifice of two mountings, with a total weight of about 60 tons. Later, two twin 25mm AA mountings were added, as well as twelve twin 13.2mm Hotchkiss AA machine-guns. The latter were carried until 1942, when six triple 25mm mountings were added, all armament and directors being situated around the flight deck edges, below deck level.
Fate: After subsidiary operations in the Philippines, Java Sea, the Bay of Bengal and the Aleutians areas, *Ryujo* joined the main Carrier Fleet in August 1942. In the Battle of the Eastern Solomons, on 24 August 1942, she was overwhelmed by aircraft from USS *Saratoga*, sustaining four 1,000lb bomb hits and a single torpedo hit. The unarmoured *Ryujo* immediately caught fire from end to end of the hangar structure and had to be abandoned, foundering some six hours after the attack.

Ryujo (1942)

Displacement tonnage	
Standard	10,600
Full load	13,650 (approx)
Dimensions	
Length (oa)	590ft 4in (179.9m)
Beam (wl)	68ft 2in (20.8m)
Draught	23ft 3in (7.08m)
Flight deck	513ft 5in (156.5m) × 75ft 6in (23m)
Hangars (both)	336ft (102.4m) × 62ft 2in (19m) approx
Arrester wires	6
Lifts	2 – largest 36ft 5in (11.1m) × 51ft 6in (15.7m)
Aircraft stowage	37 max operational
Machinery	2 sets geared turbines; 2 shafts
shp	66,270
speed	29 knots
oil fuel	2,900 tons approx
radius	10,000nm (11,500 stm = 18,425km) at 14 knots
Armament	4 × 2 127mm (5-in) DP 22 × 25mm AA
Complement	924
Builder	Yokohama Dy Co
Launched	2 April 1931
Fitted out	Yokosuka NY
Completed	9 May 1933

Soryu

Two large carriers were approved in the 1931/32 Supplementary Programme, one of which, *Soryu* ('Grey-Blue Dragon' – Japanese name for the constellation *Ursa Major*), was laid down in 1934. Early experience with *Ryujo* had demonstrated that an effective carrier could not be designed on a minimal displacement and the new carrier was declared at 15,900 tons. This left the Japanese only 4,200 tons available for carrier construction and was one of the reasons for the Japanese withdrawal from the naval agreements, the latest of which had been signed at London in 1930. *Soryu's* design was the outcome of experience with the previous ships and demonstrated the (Japanese) ideal of a fast carrier which could carry a large number of aircraft on a lightly-built hull, intended to deal blows but not receive them.
Hull: A cruiser-type hull was employed, and for the first time in a carrier the hull: beam waterline ratio attained the 'magic figure' of 10:1, enabling the ship to take full advantage of its powerful machinery to reach a very high speed. Inevitably, on such a light hull very little armour could be worked in, being limited to one inch (25mm) over the machinery and 2.2in (55mm) over the magazines and aviation fuel tanks fore and aft. The hull was not bulged for anti-torpedo protection and waterline defence consisted of a 1.8in (46mm) belt of protective plate (Ducol Steel) outboard of the machinery and magazines, backed up by an internal anti-splinter bulkhead.
Flight Deck and Hangars: The flight deck did not run the full length of the ship and was supported fore and aft of the long hangar box by pillars. The centre section, over the box, was stressed to take a 22,000lb dynamic load, the two after lifts forming part of the stressed structure when supported by the locking system. When transferring aircraft the lifts were designed to carry an 11,000lb (5,000kg) static load. The nine arrester wires would stop a 13,200lb aircraft at relative speeds between 60 and 78 knots, the last three wires before the two barriers having the lower entry speed limitation. The starboard side island was built on an extension to starboard so that it did not encroach on the available width of the flight deck as it did in most other carriers. The two hangars extended from the after lift to just ahead of the forward, largest, lift, the upper hangar being appreciably longer. The Japanese insistence on three lifts was inspired by the desire to transfer aircraft as quickly as possible but it resulted in the loss of nearly 3,000ft^2 (276m^2) of hangar area in the midships section and the three large apertures in the upper hangar deck – the strength deck – caused high concentrations of stress, particularly around the

SORYU *seen at anchor in the Kurile Islands shortly before the outbreak of War in the Pacific.*
(SHIPS OF THE WORLD)

midship lift. Designed to carry 71 aircraft, *Soryu* actually operated 63.

Soryu enjoyed a low freeboard at flight deck level – only 42ft, which was much the same as the British 'Illustrious' class which had only one hangar deck. This was achieved at the expense of hangar overhead clearance, there being only 15ft in the upper hangar and less than 14ft in the lower, where there was only about four feet separation between the top of a Mitsubishi 'Zero' fighter's engine cowling and the deck-head, while a Nakajima 'Kate' could not be folded or spread (a not-infrequent maintenance requirement) in the upper hangar.

Machinery: The boilers and turbines installed were of the same pattern as those in the 'Mogami' class heavy cruisers, the first two of which were under construction in the same Navy Yard, at Kure. Although nearly double the tonnage of the cruisers, *Soryu* was only 2½ knots slower and when the former had to be reconstructed owing to hull weakness their advantage fell to just half a knot. *Soryu's* two funnels were in the now standard Japanese position, exhausting almost horizontally amidships, abaft the island.

Armament: Three twin 127mm DP mountings were provided on either side of the ship, below the flight deck, with one fire-control director controlling each battery – the starboard director on top of the island being capable of controlling all six mountings if necessary. Fourteen twin 25mm AA mountings comprised the close-range armament, three being installed on a platform immediately under the forward lip of the flight deck.

Completed on 29 December 1937, *Soryu* was the second 'third generation' carrier to appear, the first being USS *Yorktown* (three months earlier) and the third HMS *Ark Royal,* nearly a year later. The three navies had now worked out what their basic requirements were and had produced 'production prototypes' for the series of ships which would form the backbone of the respective carrier fleets.

SORYU *seen from 15,000 feet from a US Army Air Force B-17 early on 4 June 1942, to the north of Midway Island.* (USAF)

Soryu

Displacement tonnage	
Standard	15,900
Full load	19,800
Dimensions	
Length (oa)	746ft 6in (227.5m)
Beam (wl)	69ft 11in (21.3m)
Draught	25ft (7.62m)
Flight deck	711ft 8in (216.9m) × 85ft 4in (26m)
Hangars (upper)	562ft (171.3m) × 60ft (18m)
(lower)	467ft (142.4m) × 60ft
Arrester wires	9 (aft)
Lifts	3 – largest 37ft 9in (11.5m) × 52ft 6in (16m)
Aircraft stowage	63
Machinery	4 sets geared turbines; 4 shafts
shp	152,000
speed	34.5 knots
oil fuel	3,670 tons
radius	7,750nm (8,925 stm = 14,280km) at 18 knots
Armament	6 × 2 127mm (5-in) DP 28 × 25mm AA
Complement	1,100

Hiryu

The Japanese gave notice in 1935 that they would consider themselves no longer bound by the treaties of naval limitation after 31 December 1936. Even before this date they laid down the second carrier approved in the 1931/32 Programme – a ship which remained within the individual tonnage allowance but which, with a declared standard displacement of 17,300 tons, took the Japanese Navy 13,000 tons over the collective limit.

Hiryu (Heaven-bound Dragon) is usually referred to as a modified sistership of *Soryu,* but some of the differences were sufficiently significant for her to constitute a class on her own. The earlier ship did indeed constitute the basis of the design, but the increase in tonnage available permitted some valuable improvements, some of which were incorporated in the light of experience with *Soryu.* Completed on 5 July 1939, on the eve of the outbreak of the War in Europe. *Hiryu* was the eighth ship designed from the outset as a carrier to enter service.

Hull: By comparison with *Soryu, Hiryu's* hull was one metre (3ft 3in) broader and nearly a metre longer at the waterline. The extra beam gave a marginal increase in stability but permitted a 20% increase in fuel stowage, thus overcoming one of *Soryu's* main shortcomings – her relatively short endurance. The thickness of the armoured deck remained unchanged but the protective plate outboard of the magazines was replaced by armour up to 5.9in (150mm) thick, the aviation fuel tanks being behind the 3.5in (90mm) tapered ends. The advantages of such a half-hearted scheme of protection are difficult to see, for although the magazines were thus defended against destroyer and cruiser gunfire at point-blank range they were inadequately protected from 'plunging fire' at longer ranges (or from armour-piercing bombs), the machinery was still very vulnerable, and the partial internal anti-torpedo bulkhead system was totally inadequate.

Flight Deck and Hangars: The most obvious difference between *Soryu* and *Hiryu* was the latter's port-side island, located almost exactly amidships on a very narrow extension which was not wide enough to carry the island clear of the landing area. The length of the deck was unchanged, but the extra metre of beam led to a similar increase in the width of the flight deck and hangars: the theoretical aircraft capacity was increased by two but in practice *Hiryu* carried 63, like *Soryu.* The three lifts were all larger, the total increase in area being nearly 600ft^2 (79m^2), with a corresponding increase in the stress around the apertures in the upper hangar deck. The number of arrester wires was unchanged, but one of the more powerful units, controlling three wires, was moved forward to permit landings over the bows – a technique employed in excessively high winds, the ship steaming downwind to reduce the relative wind over the deck. Such a system was also adopted for the earlier American 'Yorktown' class and the later British armoured carriers but it was never utilised to the full for a variety of practical reasons, not least being the inability to use the barriers to stop aircraft coming from the reverse direction.

Machinery: The same 4-shaft machinery was used again, with a very slight increase in power and a slight drop in maximum speed. The funnels were slightly larger and more curved than those in *Soryu,* but they remained on the starboard side, where the trunking balanced the weight of the island on the port side; in most starboard island ships, the island and uptake arrangements were compensated by the shape of the hull, which was wider to port of the ship's axis above the water line, but in *Hiryu* the hull could be completely symmetrical.

Armament: The number of 127mm mountings was unchanged but instead of the port-side two-aft and one-forward lay-out adopted in *Soryu,* in *Hiryu* the mountings on the port side were distributed two forward and one aft, matching the starboard arrangement. Both directors were on the port side, one on top of and one immediately abaft the island, on the flight deck. Triple 25mm AA guns were

HIRYU *running initial sea trials. Note central, enlarged island, fo's'cle one deck higher than* SORYU'S *and empty 'bandstands' for triple 25mm AA mountings.*

mounted along the port deck edge and on the bow platform, while the twins on the starboard side were rearranged.

Fate: *Soryu & Hiryu* – The two ships formed Carrier Division Two and operated together continuously, achieving some of the most notable successes of the first six months of the War. On 4 June 1942, during the Battle of Midway, *Soryu* was hit by three 1,000lb bombs dropped by USS *Yorktown's* dive-bombers: uncontrollable fires spread from the hangars throughout the ship and reached the aviation fuel five hours after the attack, causing the carrier to disintegrate in a colossal explosion.

Hiryu, the flagship of the Division, was not attacked in the morning strike in which *Soryu, Akagi* and *Kaga* were accounted for and she even managed to launch two successful strikes on USS *Yorktown,* making the major contribution to the eventual sinking of the American carrier. An hour after *Soryu* had blown up, however, *Hiryu* was attacked by a dozen dive-bombers which had taken off from USS *Enterprise* and sustained four 1,000lb hits forward of the centre lift. The fires which swept the hangars were prevented from engulfing the entire ship because power was still available for fire-fighting from the undamaged machinery spaces. During the night, the engine and boiler-room personnel were at last overcome by the heat and smoke entering by way of the ventilation and boiler intake system. By dawn, the carrier was a derelict, dead in the water with fires still burning and a great section of the flight deck blown out by the explosion of the bombs. She was finally despatched by Japanese destroyer torpedoes, some 70 miles from the position in which *Soryu* had sunk.

Hiryu

Displacement tonnage	
Standard	17,300
Full load	21,900
Dimensions	
Length (oa)	746ft (227.4m)
Beam (wl)	73ft 3in (22.3m)
Draught	25ft 9in (7.84m)
Flight deck	711ft 8in (216.9m) × 88ft 7in (27m)
Hangars (upper)	562ft (171.3m) × 60ft (18m)
(lower)	467ft (142.4m) × 60ft
Arrester wires	9 – 3 forward, 6 aft
Lifts	3 – largest 42ft 8in (13m) × 52ft 6in (16m)
Aircraft stowage	64
Machinery	4 sets geared turbines; 4 shafts
shp	153,000
speed	34.3 knots
oil fuel	4,400 tons
radius	10,330nm (11,900 stm = 19,030km) at 18 knots
Armament	6 × 2 127mm (5-in) DP
	31 × 25mm AA
Complement	1,100 approx

'Shoho' class

In 1933 and 1934, the Japanese Naval Staff included in the Programmes three large, fast Submarine Support Ships which would accompany the submarine flotillas to sea and direct operations. Although it has been claimed that these vessels were designed with a view to subsequent conversion to carriers, this is considered improbable in view of the time taken to convert the first one and the need to re-engine all three when converted. The 1933 Programme ship, *Taigei,* was completed in March 1935 and immediately demonstrated so many inherent design shortcomings that work on the two 1934 Programme ships was slowed down, the first, *Tsurugisaki,* not entering service until January 1939, although she was launched in June 1935. The other, *Takasaki,* it was decided, should be converted as a light aircraft carrier and the hull was launched in June 1936.

The need to work out the new design and install new machinery, while competing for the work-force at the already stretched Yokosuka Navy Yard, and the shortage of materials combined to delay completion of the re-named *Zuiho* (Lucky Phoenix) until 27 December 1940, four and a half years after launch. As soon as the dockyard berth became available, *Tsurugisaki* moved into Yokosuka for conversion under the name *Shoho* (Luck-bringing Phoenix). The work was more extensive than that required for *Zuiho,* for the superstructure had to be dismantled down to the fo'c'sle deck before the diesel machinery could be replaced by geared turbines and any work on the aviation arrangements could commence. Nevertheless, *Shoho* was converted in twelve months, re-commissioning on 26 January 1942. The previous experience with an almost-identical ship and the priority given to carrier construction contributed in equal measure to a remarkable peace-time record.

Hull: Compared with *Ryujo,* the hull was 26m (85ft) longer and two metres (seven feet) broader, with the remarkable length to beam ratio of 11:1. Considerable attention had been paid to stability during the lengthy building periods and no attempt was made to exceed the limits of prudence by adding a second hangar deck above that built on the original fo'c'sle deck. The tonnage increased from 9,500 to 11,262 (standard), but none of the addition was armour plate.

Flight Deck and Hangar: The flight deck was completely flush, with the navigating and aircraft control positions located below the level of the deck, the bridge being at the front of the hangar box, looking ahead through the three pairs of pillars which supported the forward overhang. Eight arrester wires, of the type installed in *Soryu,* were all fitted aft and there were two barriers forward. The hangar was 90ft longer than *Ryujo's* but was considerably narrower, with a capacity of 30 aircraft. Two lifts, of unequal size, connected flight deck and hangar; both were stressed to carry 11,000lb aircraft.

Machinery: The diesel engines were replaced by turbines of the same design as those in the 'Kagero' class destroyers, the carrier's greater internal space permitting the installation of four boilers instead of the three in the destroyers. The two sets of turbines were slightly less powerful than the diesels and maximum speed was reduced from 29 to 28 knots; the cruising speed increased by four knots and the response to power changes was generally superior. Both boiler-rooms were connected to a single short funnel amidships on the starboard side.

Armament: Two twin 127mm DP mountings were installed on sponsons on either side of the ship, port and starboard batteries being controlled by their own directors, also mounted below the level of the flight deck. The original close-range AA armament consisted of four twin 25mm mountings but in *Zuiho* this was increased in 1943 to 44 barrels and in mid-1944 to 68 barrels by the addition of triple mountings. By October 1944, this formidable light AA array had been supplemented by six 28-barrelled 120mm (4.72in) rocket launchers, intended for use against dive-bombers.

Fates: *Zuiho's* after flight deck was wrecked by two 500lb bombs which hit her on 26 October 1942, during the Battle of Santa Cruz. The damage was not very severe and the ship was operational within six months, after she had worked up new aircrews. She escaped damage at the Battle of the Philippine Sea on 19 and 20 June 1944, when 69 out of the 90 aircraft carried by herself, *Chitose* and *Chiyoda* failed to return. She was carrying about 20 aircraft on 24 October 1944, when the Japanese Carrier Fleet launched its last strike off Cape Engaño and on the following day, when the American carriers counter-attacked, she had only a handful of fighters left. The first wave scored one hit but this did little damage apart from destroying her remaining aircraft and it was not until the third wave arrived, some six hours later, that she became a prime target, some 60 aircraft concentrating on her and scoring many hits with bombs and torpedoes. Most of her aviation fuel had been pumped ashore before sailing so that she did not suffer a major fire and her loss two hours after the last hit was due entirely to flooding.

Shoho was sunk on her first operation. On 7 May 1942, during the Battle of the Coral Sea, she sustained eleven 1,000 and 500lb bomb hits and up to seven torpedo hits at the hands of USS *Yorktown's* pilots and one dive-bomber crashed into the starboard deck edge, shot down by AA fire. No carrier could have withstood such punishment and the lightly built *Shoho* sank less than ten minutes after the opening of the attack – the first of twelve Japanese carriers to be sunk at sea by American carrier aircraft.

Zuiho and Shoho

Displacement tonnage		
Standard	11,262	
Full load	14,200 approx	
Dimensions		
Length (oa)	672ft (204.8m)	
Beam (wl)	59ft 8in (18.2m)	
Draught	21ft 9in (6.64m)	
Flight deck	590ft 6in (180m) × 75ft 6in (23m) *Zuiho* from 1943: 631ft 11in (192.6m) × 75ft 6in	
Hangar	406ft 10in (124m) × 59ft (18m)	
Arrester wires	6	
Lifts	2 – largest 42ft 8in (13m) × 39ft 4in (12m)	
Aircraft stowage	30	
Machinery	2 sets geared turbines; 2 shafts	
shp	52,000	
speed	28.2 knots	
fuel	2,600 tons (approx)	
radius	7,800nm (8,980 stm = 14,370km) at 18 knots	
Armament	4 × 2 127mm (5in) DP 8 – 44 – 68 × 25mm AA 6 × 28 120mm rocket launchers (1944)	
Complement	785	
Builder	Yokosuka Navy Yard	
	Zuiho	**Shoho**
Launched	19 June 1936	1 June 1935
Completed	27 December 1940	15 January 1939 (as Submarine Support Ship)
Conversion completed	—	26 January 1942
Sunk	25 October 1944	7 May 1942

ZUIHO *prepares to fly off 'Zeroes' and 'Kates' during the Battle of Santa Cruz, 26 October 1942. Part of* ZUIKAKU'S *flight desk can be seen in the foreground.*
(SHIPS OF THE WORLD)

'Shokaku' class

Ordered in 1937, *Shokaku* (Heaven-bound Crane) and *Zuikaku* (Lucky Crane) saw the Japanese designers' conception of the ideal aircraft carrier realised. Big and fast, they were heavily armed and armoured and were more than a match for any two American carriers, as they demonstrated at the Battles of the Coral Sea and Santa Cruz. Completed on 8 August and 25 September 1941, respectively, *Shokaku* and *Zuikaku* finished their work-ups just in time to take part in the Pearl Harbor raid.

Hull: In appearance, these identical sisters resembled an enlarged *Soryu,* with a proportionately bigger and squatter island and the fo'c'sle raised to upper hangar deck level. Ninety-two feet longer, they were 10,000 tons heavier at standard displacement, much of the excess being taken up with armour – 170mm (6.7in) on the main deck above the machinery, magazines and petrol stowages and 215mm (8.5in) on the waterline abreast the machinery spaces, reducing to 150mm (5.9in) outboard of the magazines. The petrol tanks were still built as part of the main structure, but in mid-1942 the air spaces were filled with concrete in an attempt to give increased protection. The hull did not have quite the same fineness as *Soryu's,* but the fore-foot was of the recently-developed bulbous form which had been found to decrease the ship's underwater 'drag', permitting higher speeds and better endurance. A rounded, heavily-flared bow and raised fo'c'sle improved sea-keeping and kept the flight deck dry in most sea conditions.

Flight Deck and Hangars: After two aberrations, in *Akagi* and *Hiryu,* the Japanese Navy now forewent any advantages which might have been gained from the presence of an island on the port side of the flight deck and built two ships intended to operate side by side with starboard islands. The three lifts were identical in size to those in *Hiryu* and the same lay-out of arrester wires – three forward and six aft – was employed; a third barrier unit was installed. Hangar area was not greatly increased and the two ships each carried only nine more aircraft than *Soryu,* with a designed capacity of only 12 more. In spite of all the additional hull armour, no protection was provided for the flight deck or hangars.

Machinery: The geared turbine machinery was essentially the same as that installed in *Soryu,* maximum power being increased by only 8,000hp. Such was the efficiency of the bulbous bow, however, the maximum speed remained over 34 knots, in spite of the greater displacement, fuller hull and seven feet increase in draught. The two equal-sized funnels on the starboard side were of a plainer design than those in either *Soryu* or *Hiryu* and were curved downwards, rather than downward sloping.

Armament: The number of 127mm DP guns was increased to 16, in twin mountings distributed two forward and two aft on each side of the hull. The four batteries each had a director, also located at the deck edge, while a fifth director, on top of the island, could control any or all of the mountings. In September 1942, *Shokaku* had a primitive air warning radar fitted above the director on the island, the first set to be fitted in any Japanese carrier. Both she and *Zuikaku* were later fitted with the standard Type 2-1 air warning and control radar. Fourteen triple 25mm AA mountings were installed when completed, ten more were added in 1943 and *Zuikaku* received a further eight in August 1944, as well as six multi-barrelled 120mm rocket launchers.

Fates: *Zuikaku* escaped damage for two and a half years, but *Shokaku* sustained heavy damage twice, on 8 May and 26 October 1942, at the Battles of the Coral Sea and Santa Cruz. Hit by two bombs on the

The downward-curved stacks seen from SHOKAKU'S *island. The smoke does not appear to be blowing across the deck so that there would be little turbulence over the round-down.*

SHOKAKU *and* ZUIKAKU *were virtually identical sisters, being enlargements of the* HIRYU *design, with starboard-side island and heavier 5-in gun armament.*
(VIA USNI)

former occasion, she put out her fires only with great difficulty and nearly capsized on the way home to Japan. Off Santa Cruz she was hit by no fewer than six 1,000lb bombs but with warning of the attack she had drained down her hangar and flight deck petrol mains and she had hardly any aircraft on board. Flight and hangar decks were wrecked but no major fires developed. Finally, on 19 June 1944 in the Philippine Sea, *Shokaku* was hit by three torpedoes fired by the US submarine *Cavalla;* the aviation fuel tanks were ruptured and fuel fires started in the hangars. The latter were brought under control but two and a half hours later petrol vapour reached the area of the fires and *Shokaku* disintegrated, possibly through a 'sympathetic detonation' of her forward magazines.

Zuikaku's immunity disappeared with the loss of her sister, for on the next day she was hit by a 500lb bomb which started a hangar fire which was extinguished hours later. Repaired, she was sunk at the Battle of Cape Engaño, on 25 October 1944, after sustaining numerous torpedo and bomb hits.

Shokaku and Zuikaku

Displacement tonnage

Standard	25,675
Full load	32,000 approx

(after the Japanese withdrew from the Naval Treaties, their calculation of 'standard tonnage' was somewhat rough and ready and the essential figures from which they worked were the Light and Trials Displacements, the latter being Full load less 33% fuel, fresh water and victualling stores; in the case of *Shokaku,* the Trials Displacement was 29,800 tons – add 1,350 tons of furnace fuel and 150 tons of aviation fuel and a figure of 31,300 tons is arrived at, leaving the unknowns of fresh water and stores tonnage to be added)

Dimensions		
Length (oa)	844ft 9in (257.5m)	
Beam (wl)	85ft 4in (26m)	
Draught	29ft 1in (8.87m)	
Flight deck	794ft 7in (242.2m) × 95ft 2in (26m)	
Hangars (upper)	623ft (190m) × 78ft (24m)	
(approx) (lower)	525ft (160m) × 78ft	
Arrester wires	3 forward, 6 aft	
Lifts	3 – largest 42ft 8in (13m) × 52ft 7in (16m)	
Aircraft stowage	72	
Machinery	4 sets geared turbines; 4 shafts	
shp	160,000	
speed	34.2 knots	
fuel	4,100 tons	
radius	9,700nm (11,170 stm = 17,870km) at 18 knots	
Armament	8 × 2 127mm (5-in) DP 42 – 72 – 96 × 25mm AA 6 × 28 120mm rocket launchers (1944 – *Zuikaku*)	
Complement	1,660	
	Shokaku	**Zuikaku**
Builder	Yokosuka NY	Kawasaki, Kobe
Launched	1 June 1939	27 November 1939
Completed	8 August 1941	25 September 1941
Sunk	19 June 1944	24 October 1944

'Junyo' class

In August 1940 the Imperial Japanese Navy requisitioned two large merchant hulls on the stocks. These two ships were to have been 27,500 grt, 24 knot passenger liners – instead they became the 24,140 (standard) ton, 53-aircraft carriers *Junyo* (Free-flying Falcon) and *Hiyo* (Peregrine Falcon). The most elaborate merchant conversions attempted, apart from the Italian *Aquila,* they were intended for Fleet use and were fitted out to the standard of the earlier large carriers. Visually, they were notable for introducing the combined island-and-funnel lay-out to Japanese carriers. Their completion in the summer of 1942, *Junyo* on 5 May and *Hiyo* on 31 July, was opportune, but they proved to be no real substitutes for the four ships lost at Midway on 4 June.

Hull: The external form of the liner hull was unchanged, as was the line of the fo'c'sle, but the early stage at which conversion began allowed the lower hangar deck to built on the deck above the machinery rooms, with the usual sheer and camber eliminated. Seven-tenths of a metre (2ft 9in) beamier and nearly 35m (114ft) shorter than *Shokaku, Junyo* and *Hiyo* were inherently more stable and did not require bulging for stability, although they might have benefited from the anti-torpedo protection. The only armour fitted was light plating over the magazines and the internal sub-division was regarded as being inferior to that in contemporary purpose-built carriers.

Flight Deck and Hangars: The steel plate flight deck had an area at least as great as that of *Soryu,* being slightly shorter but over a metre (four feet) wider. Six wires were rigged aft and three forward, fore and aft of the forward lift and abreast the island; the last forward wire was also used to provide the tension in a light barrier which could be rigged to protect the after deck park from aircraft landing over the bows. Two 46 × 46ft lifts, with the standard 5,000kg (11,000lb) limitation, served the upper and lower hangars. Overhead clearance in the hangars was less than in other Japanese carriers, the lower being barely ten feet high and suitable only for fighter aircraft; ventilation in the lower hangar was reputed to be very poor and the ambient temperature high due to the inadequate air space between the boiler uptakes and the casing which passed up the starboard hangar wall.

Machinery: The most unsatisfactory feature of the class was the main machinery. In order to increase maximum power to obtain an extra 1½ knots, the commercial-type boilers were removed and destroyer boilers installed. The marriage between the original geared turbines and the new boilers was not a success and the early career of the ships was

The largest carrier to be converted from a merchant hull, JUNYO *lies at Sasebo after the surrender of Japan. All armament has been removed, but the antennae of the Type 2-1 and 1-3 radars have been left, the former on top of the island and on the port quarter and the latter on the mainmast.* (US NAVY)

plagued with mechanical breakdowns. To make matters worse, the power was still insufficient to move such broad, relatively deep-draught ships at their designed maximum speed and the sea speed of 22 knots was not enough to enable them to operate satisfactorily in company with even the converted light Fleet carriers. The number of aircraft which could be flown off at a time was limited by the strength of the wind – a disadvantage which would have been unimportant if there was a catapult.

If the main machinery was not a success, then at least the new funnel arrangement was. The stack was angled outwards, to carry smoke well clear of the deck, and it was much taller than in the ships of the Western navies. The advantages of the island-mounted funnel were fully appreciated by the Japanese, but they were able to incorporate it in only two more designs.

Armament: Six twin 127mm DP mountings were installed, with two 'sided' directors to control the fire of the six-gun batteries on either side or take charge of all 12 guns to cover one another's blind arcs. Eight triple 25mm AA guns were mounted initially, but more triples and singles were added to bring the total to 40 barrels in 1943 and 76 (plus six rocket launchers) in *Junyo* in the autumn of 1944. Type 1-3 air-warning radar was installed on the mainmast and Type 2-1 warning and aircraft control radar on the island in 1943/4, *Junyo* featuring a second Type 2-1 in a cabin on the port side of the flight deck, right aft – a somewhat hazardous location subsequently much favoured by the Japanese.

Fates: *Hiyo* was hit by a torpedo fired by the US submarine *Trigger* on the night of 10/11 June 1943, some 180 miles south of Tokyo Bay. Although badly damaged, she was in no serious danger and was repaired within four months. In the Battle of the Philippine Sea, the American carrier strike on 20 June 1944 scored two bomb hits on *Junyo,* holing the flight deck abaft the island but inflicting no serious damage. *Hiyo* was hit by a torpedo, suffering damage to her petrol tanks: the vapour spread through the ship, finally igniting two hours after the hit. The force of the explosion was such that the Japanese were convinced that she had been hit by another torpedo which had started uncontrollable fires. *Hiyo* rolled over and sank shortly after the explosion – the third Japanese carrier to be lost to the same combination of torpedo damage and petrol vapour explosion in 36 hours.

Junyo was repaired but was not sent out on the sortie which ended with the death of the Japanese carrier Fleet off Cape Engaño late October 1944. Instead, she was used for training and aircraft transport duties in Home Waters and the East China Sea. It was while she was thus engaged that she was torpedoed by the American submarine USS *Redfish* off Nagasaki on 9 December 1944. She survived the severe damage, probably because her petrol stowage and bomb magazines were empty, and was laid up after repairs. Captured at the end of the war, she was set to work as a Repatriation Transport until 1947, when she was sent to Sasebo to be scrapped.

Junyo (ex-Kashiwara Maru) and Hiyo (ex-Izumo Maru)

Displacement tonnage		
Standard	24,140	
Full load	28,300 (approx)	
Dimensions		
Length (oa)	719ft 6in (219.3m)	
Beam (wl)	87ft 7in (26.7m)	
Draught	26ft 9in (8.15m)	
Flight deck	690ft (210.3m) × 89ft 7in (27.3m)	
Hangars (upper)	557ft 9in (170m) × 82ft (24m)	
approx (lower)	452ft (138m) × 82ft	
Arrester wires	3 forward, 6 aft	
Lifts	2 – largest 46ft (14m) × 46ft	
Aircraft stowage	53	
Machinery	2 sets geared turbines; 2 shafts	
shp	56,250	
speed	25.5 knots designed, 22.5 max sea speed	
fuel	2,800 tons approx	
radius	c 7,500nm (8,630 stm = 13,800km) at 16 knots	
Armament	6 × 2 127mm (5-in) DP 24 – 40 – 76 × 25mm AA 6 × 28 120mm rocket launchers (1944 – *Junyo*)	
Complement	1,187-1,224	
	Junyo	**Hiyo**
Builder	Mitsubishi, Nagasaki	Kawasaki, Kobe
Launched	26 June 1941	24 June 1941
Completed	5 May 1942	31 July 1942
Sunk	—	20 June 1944

Ryuho

Reference has already been made to the Submarine Support Ship *Taigei* (see 'Shoho' class) and her shortcomings. Space does not allow the recounting of the defects and the steps taken to ameliorate the worst deficiences of a frightful design. Even after major alteration, *Taigei* was still only barely satisfactory and by 1940 the concept of the submarine control ship did not seem to offer the tactical advantages promised in the early '30s. It was therefore decided that she should be converted as a light carrier and, renamed *Ryuho* (Dragon-Phoenix) she was taken in hand at Yokosuka early in 1941.

Hull: The superstructure was raised to the deck above the fo'c'sle deck, the hangar and flight deck being built above. The ship's keel had already been strengthened in the 1936/7 reconstruction and to increase the girder strength still more, the Japanese built the flight deck as the strength deck, using heavy longitudinals extending from the navigating bridge under the forward overhang to the after end of the single-storey hangar. Freeboard at the flight deck was reduced to 40ft, from the original amidship height of 42ft, and with draught increased by 1.33m (4½ft) by raising the standard tonnage from 10,000 to 13,360, combined with the bulges added in 1936/7, *Ryuho* was stronger and more stable than even the reconstructed *Taigei.* No armour was built into the hull, the thickness of the decks being a uniform 10mm, and the internal sub-division was poor by any standard.

Flight Deck and Hangar: Like *Shoho, Ryuho* was flush-decked, the surface being wood planking over the steel beams. The deck was only five metres (16ft) longer than *Shoho's,* a generous length of open fo'c'sle being left; as in *Zuiho,* the deck was extended in 1943 to enable the ship to operate heavier aircraft. The weight limitations on the two large lifts and the six arrester wires remained the same as in earlier carriers. The hangar extended from the back of the accommodation and 'offices' which had been under the original bridge to the rear end of the 'box' and had operational stowage for 31 aircraft.

Machinery: The 14,000hp diesel engines were stripped out and replaced by 52,000hp destroyer machinery driving two shafts. Speed was thus increased from 20 to 26½ knots, but this was not realised at sea in loaded condition and *Ryuho* was therefore teamed-up with *Junyo* and *Hiyo.* The funnel arrangement was similar to that in *Shoho,* a single stack exhausting amidships on the starboard side, emerging a fraction lower than in the smaller ship.

Armament: The main DP armament was the standard two pairs of twin 127mm mountings, the four guns on each side being controlled by their own director, mounted below the flight deck. Twelve triple and two single 25mm AA mountings were gradually augmented until by June 1944 *Ryuho* was carrying 61 × 25mm barrels. Space was later found for six 120mm rocket launchers and 14 twin 13.2mm AA machine guns. In 1944, a Type 2-1 warning and control radar was installed on the port side of the flight deck, aft.

RYUHO *lying derelict near Kure after the end of the war.* (US NAVY)

Fate: *Ryuho* completed her conversion on 28 November 1942. That she was a disappointment to the Imperial Japanese Navy in her second incarnation as well as her first is clear: since May 1942, four large and two light carriers had been sunk and only three ships, with a total aircraft capacity of 166 aircraft, had been completed yet *Ryuho* was not allocated to a Carrier Division until June 1943, and then only to replace the damaged *Hiyo.* The intervening six months had been occupied in training aircrew in the waters around Japan.

Ryuho's only operation was that which led up to the Battle of the Philippine Sea, in which she sustained only slight damage from near-miss bombs. Thereafter she was laid up at Kure, fully manned and operational but without aircraft. On 19 March 1945 she was attacked by American carrier aircraft and was hit by three bombs and two 5-in rockets. Two bombs detonated in the hangar and their cumulative blast bulged the flight deck upwards into an arch six feet high between the lifts. The third bomb penetrated the thin decks and plates and exploded after travelling 60 feet, blowing a 25-ft diameter hole in the port side aft, below the waterline. The underwater damage was patched up and the ship decommissioned on 20 April 1945. She was not attacked again and was scrapped at Kure in 1946-47.

Ryuho

Displacement tonnage	
Standard	13,360
Full load	16,700 approx
Dimensions	
Length (oa)	707ft 4in (215.6m)
Beam (wl)	64ft 3in (19.58m)
Draught	21ft 11in (6.67m)
Flight deck	607ft (185m) × 75ft 6in (23m) 1943: 660ft 11in (210.4m) × 75ft 6in
Hangar (approx)	407ft (124m) × 61ft (18.6m)
Arrester wires	6
Lifts	2 – largest 44ft 8in (13.6m) × 39ft 8in (12m)
Aircraft stowage	31
Machinery	2 sets geared turbines; 2 shafts
shp	52,000
speed	26.5 knots
fuel	2,900 tons approx
radius	8,000nm (9,200 stm = 14,740km) at 18 knots
Armament	4 × 2 127mm (5-in) DP 38 – 42 – 61 × 25mm AA 6 – 28 × 13.2mm AA 6 × 28 120mm rocket launchers (1944)
Complement	989
Builder	Yokosuka NY
Launched	16 November 1933
Completed	31 March 1935 (as 'Submarine Support Ship)
Conversion	1941-2 at Yokosuka NY
Completed	28 November 1942

'Chitose' class

One of the means adopted by the Japanese to minimise the effects of Treaty limits on carrier tonnage was the development of long-range floatplanes for Fleet reconnaissance duties, in order to free the carrier aircraft for the strike and air defence roles. Following experience with two large converted tankers, the Imperial Japanese Navy ordered two 11,000-ton seaplane carriers which would carry up to 24 short-range observation and long-range reconnaissance floatplanes. *Chitose* (named for a city on Hokkaido) and *Chiyoda* (poetic title of the Imperial Palace, Tokyo) were laid down in 1934 and, completed in 1938, represented the ultimate in this type of design. The armament and accommodation were concentrated in the forward third of the ship, immediately ahead of the unusual combined diesel and steam turbine machinery, and the after part was given over to seaplane stowage and handling space, with no fewer than six cranes (booms) around a flat-topped but open sided shelter amidships and a seventh on the stern, and an elaborate trolley track system for manoeuvring aircraft between the electric lift and the four catapults. Below decks, there were a long hangar in which aircraft were stowed athwartships on their trollies, aviation workshops and stores. With a maximum speed of just under 29 knots, the two ships were capable of operations with the Fleet and had a range greater than that of any of the carriers. Typically, the Japanese could not let well alone, and in 1941 both ships were modified to carry and launch, of all things, midget submarines, large hatches being cut in the stern and aircraft capacity reduced by half.

Both ships served as carrier-surrogates in the Philippines and East Indies during the opening months of the War and *Chitose's* aircraft saw action during the Midway operation, before the ship was relegated to transport duties. *Chitose* sustained severe damage at the Battle of Santa Cruz in October 1942 and after repairs had begun, in November it was decided to convert her as a light carrier. *Chiyoda* was taken in hand in early 1943 and, thanks to the preliminary drawing work being already complete, she was re-commissioned on 31 October 1943, a day before *Chitose.*

Hull: The hull was levelled to the fo'c'sle deck and the hangar and flight deck built above, after the fashion of *Shoho.* To compensate for the extra topweight, large bulges increased the beam by two metres (six and a half feet), while the waterline length was increased by the same amount in the interests of maintaining the fineness.

Flight Deck and Hangars: The flight deck was the same length as *Shoho's* and as wide, but the taper forward was more pronounced. Two lifts, the for-

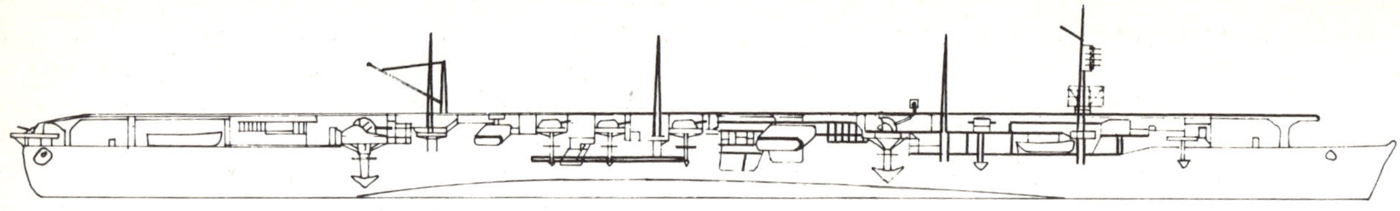

CHITOSE *as converted (1944).*

ward one hexagonal and the after one octagonal, and the six arrester wires were all designed to the usual standards. The original lower half-length hangar was retained, served by the new after lift, as only half the ship's length could be devoted to the provision of an upper hangar. With a standard displacement of only 11,200 tons, the 'Chitose' class were the smallest two-hangar ships ever converted. Aircraft complement was identical to that of *Zuiho,* with whom they formed the 3rd Carrier Division in February 1944. Too small to operate the Navy's dive-bombers, they were instead armed with 15 Mitsubishi 'Zero' fighter-bombers, six standard 'Zero' interceptors and nine Nakajima 'Kate' or 'Jill' torpedo-bombers.

Machinery: The original two-shaft geared turbine/diesel installation was overhauled but not replaced and even after the alterations to the hull the speed fell by only a fraction of a knot. The boiler uptakes were led to a small downwards pointing stack amidships while the diesel exhausts, which had formerly been located in the uprights of the seaplane shelter, now had a single 'baby' stack abaft the steam and smoke stack.

Armament: The usual two pairs of twin 127mm DP mountings and 'sided' directors were installed around the sides of the upper hangar deck, as were 10 triple 25mm AA mountings; the close-range armament was increased to 16 triple mountings in July 1944.

Fates: *Chiyoda,* the flagship of CarDiv 3, was hit aft by a 500lb bomb on 20 June 1944: fires were started in the hangar and on the flight deck but these quickly brought under control, probably because she had no aircraft in the hangar, the fuel mains had been drained down and the foam spray system in the hangar was still operative.

On 25 October 1944, both ships were hit by bombs off Cape Engaño. *Chitose* sank within an hour as the result of flooding caused mainly by near-misses but *Chiyoda* remained afloat with her uncontrollable fires. Left behind by the remnant of the Fleet, she was finished off by US cruiser gunfire.

Chitose and Chiyoda

Displacement tonnage		
Standard	11,190	
Full load	15,300 approx	
Dimensions		
Length (oa)	631ft 6in (192.5m)	
Beam (wl)	68ft 3in (20.8m)	
Draught	24ft 8in (7.5m)	
Flight deck	590ft 7in (180m) × 75ft 6in (23m)	
Hangars (upper)	328ft (100m) × 59ft (18m)	
approx (lower)	197ft (60m) × 42ft 8in (13m)	
Arrester wires	6	
Lifts	2 – forward 42ft 8in (13m) × 39ft 3in (12m) (upper hangar only); after 41ft (12.5m) × 39ft 3in (both hangars)	
Aircraft stowage	30	
Machinery	2 sets geared turbines, 2 diesel engines; 2 shafts	
shp	Turbines 44,000, diesels 12,800	
speed	28.9 knots	
fuel	3,000 tons (approx) furnace fuel and diesel oil	
radius	11,000nm (12,660 stm = 20,250km) at 18 knots	
Armament	4 × 2 127mm (5-in) DP 30 – 48 × 25mm AA	
Complement	800 approx	
Builder	Kure NY	
	Chitose	**Chiyoda**
Launched	29 November 1936	19 November 1937
Completed (as Seaplane carriers)	25 July 1938	15 December 1938
Conversion	Sasebo NY	Yokosuka NY
Completed	1 November 1943	31 October 1943
Sunk	25 October 1944	25 October 1944

Taiho

The last Japanese carrier design to be initiated before the war represented a radical change in emphasis, in that the ship was not only to be able to deliver hard blows, by means of her aircraft, but was to be able to withstand them, too. With no limitations on the displacement of the ship, the designers were able to provide an armoured flight deck and hull, intended to allow the ship to continue fighting after being hit, as opposed to merely surviving. Ordered in 1939, her design was clearly influenced by the knowledge that the British were building armoured carriers, the value of which had been demonstrated by the time that *Taiho* (Great Phoenix) was laid down in 1941.

Hull: The Japanese scheme of armour was not the same as that adopted by the British for the "Illustrious' class. Whereas the latter made the hangar an armoured box, with sides and ends at least as thick as the flight deck, the Japanese provided only an armoured lid, between 75 and 80mm (2.95-3.14-in) thick, extending between the two lifts. The upper hangar deck was unarmoured and the lower was of 32mm (1.25in). The thickness of the waterline belt varied between 55mm (2.2in) abreast the machinery and 152mm (6in) outside the magazines. Internal torpedo protection was provided ten feet inboard of the outer plating and consisted of a 40mm anti-splinter steel bulkhead. The aviation petrol tanks fore and aft were only partially protected by the main armour and the only concession to wartime experience was the filling of the air space around the tanks with concrete, which gave only minimal protection against splinters and filled up the only 'overflow' available if the tanks were to be split.

The effect of the weight of the armour was to immerse the hull so deeply that the lower hangar deck was barely above the load waterline and the bottom of the lift wells, which formed part of the roofs of the petrol tanks, were actually below the waterline.

The Japanese also adopted the enclosed bow in *Taiho,* extending the hull plating up to the flight deck to improve seaworthiness and airflow over the forward end of the deck.

Flight Deck and Hangars: The usual factor of strength – twice the load of the heaviest aircraft to be embarked – did not need to be applied to *Taiho* with her immensely strong deck, but the lifts were designed to carry heavier loads than in earlier ships, up to 7,500kg (16,500lb). The arrester wires – six forward and eight aft – were of the proven 13,200lb/78 knots type; two barriers were located abreast the after end of the island and one at the forward end, the latter for use with the forward wires. Only two lifts could be installed, at the fore and aft ends of the two hangars, as the platforms could not be armoured and it was undesirable to weaken the integrity of the armoured flight deck amidships. The designed aircraft capacity was 84, but maximum usable complement was nearer 60 as the Imperial Japanese Navy did not insist on its aircraft having the smallest possible folded span and the Yokosuka D4Y 'Judy' dive-bombers carried by *Taiho* in 1944 did not have folding wings at all!

Machinery: *Taiho* had the most powerful machinery ever installed in a Japanese warship, exceeding the designed 160,000hp by 20,000hp to propel her at 33.34 knots over the measured mile, at a trials displacement of 28,300 tons. The boiler uptakes were trunked into a single large funnel on the island, canted out to starboard as in the 'Junyo' class.

Armament: The calibre of the main gun armament was changed for the first time since 1933 and the number of barrels was reduced once again to 12. The gun was the new 100mm (3.9-in) Type 98 AA gun – an excellent weapon which was installed in pairs in enclosed gun-houses, three on either side of the ship. One director was sited on the flight deck ahead of the island and the other on the port side amidships, below the level of the flight deck. Fifteen triple 25mm AA mountings were installed around the sponsons and under the after round-down and one was fitted on the flight deck in front of the island – an unusual position in a Japanese carrier. Two air warning and control radars were fitted, one above the bridge and the other behind the funnel, on the island.

Fate: *Taiho* was completed on 7 March 1944, worked up at Singapore for six weeks after sea trials and then spent a month in enforced and unproductive idleness awaiting the decisive battle in the Pacific, in the Philippine Sea. On 19 June 1944 she was hit by a single torpedo fired by the American submarine USS *Albacore.* The explosion, abreast the forward lift, split the forward petrol tanks and as the ship trimmed five feet by the bows due to flooding so the lift well filled with a mixture of sea water and petrol which had seeped up through cracks in the concrete. The danger presented by the volatile vapour was readily appreciated by the damage control personnel, but their countermeasures were lacking in commonsense, reflecting the lack of training in the short time since commissioning. Portable pumps could not keep pace with the ingress of fuel and water in the lift well but no attempt was made to cover the lethal brew with foam from the hangar system. Normal ventilation of the hangar by means of the natural draught between the lifts was not possible as the forward lift

TAIHO *at anchor south of Singapore during her 1944 work-up. The rake of the funnel is not apparent in this beam view in which she resembles a British Fleet carrier.* (US NAVY)

had jammed between decks and the hole in the flight deck had been planked over with zealous efficiency by the flight deck damage control party; it was therefore decided to open all hangar doors and hatches, thus permeating the entire ship with a heavy petrol vapour. Permeation was increased to saturation by the despairing but singularly stupid decision of the Damage Control Officer to switch on all mechanical ventilation throughout the ship to clear the fumes. Up to this point the ship was in danger, but thereafter she was doomed, only a spark being needed to create a monstrous explosion. Five hours after the torpedo hit, *Taiho* blew up, the blast blowing out the unarmoured hangar walls and part of the ship's side below the waterline and splitting the flight deck armour, which had apparently deflected much of the blast downwards, down the centre. The 'Great Phoenix' still did not sink immediately, a further hour and a half passing before she finally capsized, taking over 1,000 of her crew. The ultimate product of Japanese carrier experience had been needlessly lost through the ineptitude of her damage control personnel.

Taiho

Displacement tonnage	
Standard	29,300
Full load	37,270
Dimensions	
Length (oa)	854ft 8in (260.5m)
Beam (wl)	90ft 11in (27.7m), 110ft 3in (33.6m) max
Draught	31ft 5in (9.6m)
Flight deck	844ft 10in (257.5m) × 98ft 5in (30m)
Hangars	500ft (152.6m) × 74ft (22.5m) (between lifts)
Arrester wires	6 forward, 8 aft
Lifts	2 – largest 45ft 11in (14m) × 45ft 11in
Aircraft stowage	60-63
Machinery	4 sets geared turbines; 4 shafts
shp	180,000
speed	33.3 knots
fuel	5,700 tons
radius	10,000nm (11,515 stm = 18,400km) at 18 knots
Armament	6 × 2 100mm (3.93-in) AA 45 × 25mm AA
Complement	1,751
Builder	Kawasaki, Kobe
Launched	7 April 1943
Completed	7 March 1944
Sunk	19 June 1944

'Unryu' class

Once the Japanese Government had decided upon a policy that would almost certainly lead to war with the United States, the Navy drew up a 'War Construction Programme' that included six aircraft carriers for the main Fleet. Considerations of ease of manufacture and availability of materials led to the adoption of a standard design based on that of *Hiryu*, rather than that of *Shokaku* or *Taiho*, both of which required considerable amounts of armour plate and special machinery. The first three ships were laid down shortly after the beginning of the War and the second three in 1943, the delay being accounted for by the lack of suitable slipways. Eleven more ships of the same class were ordered in 1942, as well as eight 'Taiho' class, but even the Imperial Naval Staff must have realised that Japan's shipbuilding industry lacked the resources for such ambitious programmes and these ships were never laid down. Indeed, of the six ships laid down, two had to be re-engined with destroyer turbines as the cruiser-type machinery could not be supplied within the prescribed time-scale; even then, only three ships were commissioned before construction was suspended in 1945.

Hull: The hull was almost identical to that of *Hiryu*, with the same distribution of armour. The weight of the island, moved back to the starboard side of the flight deck had to be compensated by increasing the width of the hull above the waterline to port. Extensive welding was not employed.

Flight Deck and Hangars: The starboard-side island was considerably larger than *Hiryu's*, to accommodate the extra 'offices', but, like *Soryu's*, it did not encroach on the width of the flight deck. The amidships lift was omitted, to preserve the integrity of the strength deck (upper hangar), and a completely new type of pentagonal platform was provided for the after lift, the loading remaining that of the earlier ships – 11,000lb. The three arrester wires and one barrier forward and six wires and two barriers aft were the well-tried Type 3 units, with the 13,200lb limitation. Aviation fuel capacity was halved, to 48,000 Imp galls, after battle experience had shown that those carriers which had been lost through fuel fires had had time to use only a small proportion of their petrol before being hit. The air space around the integral tanks was filled with con-

UNRYU *after commissioning, autumn 1944. The raised fo'c'sle of* **HIRYU** *and large island of* **SHOKAKU** *have been combined to produce an 'improved Soryu'.*

crete, as in *Taiho.*

Machinery: *Unryu* and *Amagi,* like the uncompleted *Kasagi* and *Ikoma,* were fitted with the same 152,000hp machinery as *Soryu* and *Hiryu,* but the Kure Navy Yard was obliged to make do with two complete sets of destroyer turbines, driving four shafts, with a maximum output of 104,000hp, for *Katsuragi* and *Aso;* in fact, the lower-powered ships were not greatly handicapped, *Katsuragi* making 32.7 knots on trials at a displacement of nearly 21,000 tons.

Armament: The six twin 127mm DP mountings were laid out like those of *Hiryu,* but the only director was mounted on the island, where its astern arc was partially masked by the main-mast. The original close-range armament of *Unryu* and *Amagi* consisted of 16 triple and three single 25mm AA mountings and it is believed that this was later augmented, to as many as 89 barrels, in addition to the six 28-barrelled AA rocket launchers. Ranging radar was fitted to the main gunnery director, a Type 1-3 air warning radar was installed on the mainmast, and there was a Type 2-1 warning and control radar on the port side of the flight deck, right aft.

Fates: *Unryu* (Heavenward-bound Dragon riding the Clouds) was commissioned on 6 August 1944 and allocated to the 1st Carrier Division as was her sister-ship *Amagi* (named after an extinct volcano) when she was completed five days later. Shortage of aircraft and crews following the Battle of the Philippine Sea resulted in priority for equipment going to carriers which were already operating, but *Unryu* embarked some aircraft for convoy escort duties in the autumn. It was while she was thus engaged that she was torpedoed by the American submarine USS *Redfish* in the East China Sea on 19 December 1944. The torpedoes struck in the vicinity of the forward bomb magazines and petrol stowage and the ship sank very quickly, leaving few survivors, after a huge explosion.

Katsuragi (a mountain near Osaka) joined the same Carrier Division on completion on 15 October 1944 and, like *Amagi,* did not embark aircraft for operations or even leave Kure after the beginning of 1945, due to the lack of fuel. On 24 July 1945, both ships were hit by 2,000lb bombs which exploded in their hangars, wrecking the centre-section of the flight decks. *Amagi* also sustained severe underwater splinter damage which led to her capsizing in shallow water. *Katsuragi* was made weather-proof after the surrender and was used for repatriation duties until November 1946, when she went to Osaka for scrapping.

Unryu and Amagi

Displacement tonnage		
Standard	17,150 (*Unryu*), 17,460 (*Amagi*)	
Full load	22,400 (*Unryu*), 22,800 (*Amagi*) – both approx	
Dimensions		
Length (oa)	745ft 11in (227.4m)	
Beam (wl)	72ft 2in (22m)	
Draught	25ft 9in (7.85m)	
Flight deck	711ft 7in (216.9m) × 88ft 7in (27m)	
Hangars (upper)	574ft (175m) × 68ft 11in (21m)	
(lower)	426ft 6in (130m) × 68ft 11in	
Arrester wires	3 forward, 6 aft	
Lifts	2 – largest 45ft 11in (14m) × 45ft 11in	
Aircraft stowage	63	
Machinery	4 sets geared turbines; 4 shafts	
shp	152,000	
speed	34 knots (designed)	
fuel	3,670 tons	
radius	8,000nm (9,200 stm = 14,740km) at 18 knots	
Armament	6 × 2 127mm (5-in) DP	
	89 × 25mm AA	
	6 × 28 120mm rocket launchers	
Complement	1,595	
	Unryu	*Amagi*
Builders	Yokosuka NY	Mitsubishi, Nagasaki
Launched	25 September 1943	15 October 1943
Completed	6 August 1944	11 August 1944
Sunk	19 December 1944	24 July 1945

Uncompleted sister ships
Kasagi (Mitsubishi, Nagasaki) launched 19 October 1944
Ikoma (Kawasaki, Kobe) launched 17 November 1944

Katsuragi as *Unryu,* except:

Displacement tonnage	
Standard	17,260
Full load	22,534
Dimensions	
Draught	25ft 5in (7.76m)
Flight deck	703ft 9in (214.5m) × 88ft 7in
Machinery	4 sets geared turbines; 4 shafts
shp	104,000
speed	32.7 knots (trials)
Complement	1,500
Builder	Kure NY
Launched	19 January 1944
Completed	15 October 1944

Uncompleted sister-ship *Aso* (Kure NY) launched 1 November 1944

Shinano

The biggest carrier ever to be built outside the United States, *Shinano* (former name of a Japanese province) was laid down in 1940 as the third battleship of the 'Yamato' class. Construction was halted in the autumn of 1941, and, after the Battle of Midway, plans were prepared for her completion as a carrier. Her intended role was stated at the end of the War to have been that of a support ship, operating in a rear area to provided reserve aircraft, fuel and ordnance for the front-line carriers, with only 47 of her own aircraft embarked.

Hull: The original hull, up to the undulating line of the fo'c'sle deck, was retained, all above that deck being razed or omitted. The belt armour thickness was halved to 205mm (8.1in) compared with the battleships, but the armoured deck over the machinery and magazines remained 190mm (7.5in) thick (and not 200mm as in many sources). Below the waterline, the first line of anti-torpedo defence was a deep bulge, behind which was a thick armoured bulkhead, joined to and extending down from the belt armour, to stop splinters; model tests had indicated that the bulkhead was not watertight but there was a sandwich-type watertight bulkhead behind. In spite of the removal of the three triple 457mm (17.99in) turrets and barbettes, as well as half the thickness of the belt armour, *Shinano's* trials displacement, at 67,123 tons, was only 2,800 tons less than that of *Yamato* (69,935).

Flight Deck and Hangar: Much of the saving in hull and turret armour was lost in the erection of a flight deck with armour 80mm (3.14in) thick between the two lifts. As in *Taiho*, this formed a lid to an otherwise unarmoured hangar which was 111ft wide forward and had a minimum width of 65ft aft. Only one hangar deck, 16½ft high, could be provided for stability reasons and this followed the line of the original fo'c'sle, with considerable sheer forward but reasonably level abaft the island. The hangar sides were not plated over in part of the forward section, the freeboard of nearly 20ft and the flare of the bows being sufficient to keep the sea out, while steel shutters could be made almost 'light-tight'. This forward section could be used for engine test runs and the whole area was to be given over to maintenance and storage. The two lifts had the same capacity as *Taiho's*, 7,500kg (16,500lb), and the 15 arrester wires and three barriers (six wires and a barrier forward) were the standard Type 3 units. Although by 1944 it was intended that she should operate only 47 aircraft of her own, her fore and aft petrol tanks, surrounded by concrete, had a maximum capacity of 158,000 Imp galls (190,000 US galls = 718,700 litres).

Machinery: The 150,000 steam turbine machinery was the same as that in *Yamato*. With a fractionally reduced draught, it is probable that *Shinano* would have exceeded her 'step-sister's' 27.7 knots had she run trials. The uptakes from the 12 boilers were led to an enormous angled funnel on top of the largest island to appear on a Japanese carrier.

Armament: Eight twin 127mm DP mountings were arranged in four batteries, those on the port side being adjacent to their fire control directors while directors on extensions fore and aft of the island controlled the starboard guns and the entire forward and after batteries when necessary. Thirty-three triple 25mm mountings and 12 multi-barrelled rocket launchers were fitted for close-range defence. Two Type 1-3 warning radars were installed, one on the mainmast and one on a hinged mast on the port side forward; there were also two aircraft control radars on the island.

Fate: *Shinano* commissioned on 18 November 1944 and sailed for Kure ten days later, apparently to avoid air attacks on the Tokyo area. The crew was not yet familiar with the ship, the watertightness of the armoured 'citadel' had not been tested, the packing around cable runs and pipes passing through bulkheads was not complete and many of the counter-flooding and damage control pumps had not been delivered. In the early hours of 29 November *Shinano* was hit by four torpedoes fired by USS *Archerfish*. The elaborate armoured and sandwich bulkhead system was completely defeated and although the initial list of 10° was checked by counter-flooding, the lack of pumps, inadequate internal watertightness and poor damage control procedures allowed the flooding to spread; after

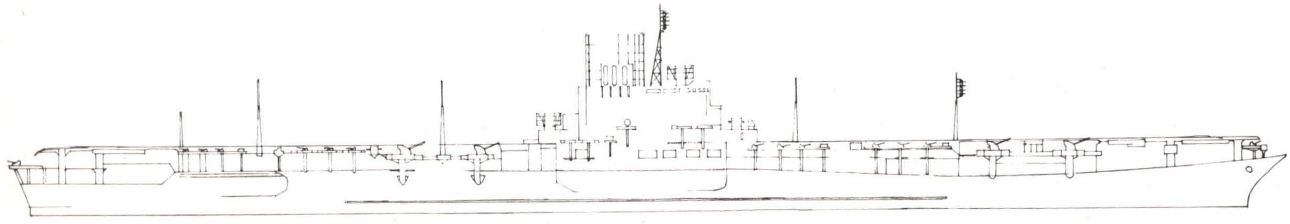

SHINANO *as completed (1944).*

two and a half hours all power was lost when the boilers rooms had flooded. Five hours later, *Shinano* capsized to starboard and sank. In the words of the Official US Navy Technical Report: 'the shock which went through the Japanese Naval Ministry is better imagined than described.'

Shinano

Displacement tonnage	
Standard	64,800
Full load	71,890 (calculated by US Navy)
Dimensions	
Length (oa)	872ft 9in (266m)
Beam (wl)	119ft 1in (36.3m)
Draught	33ft 10in (10.3m)
Flight deck	839ft 11in (256m) × 131ft 3in (40m)
Hangar	536ft (163m) × 111ft (33.8m) approx
Arrester wires	6 forward, 9 aft
Lifts	2 – largest 49ft 3in (15m) × 45ft 11in (14m)
Aircraft stowage	47+aircraft in reserve and undergoing maintenance
Machinery	4 sets geared turbines; 4 shafts
shp	150,000 (designed)
speed	27 knots (designed)
fuel	8,900 tons
radius	10,000nm (11,515 stm = 18,400km) at 18 knots (designed)
Armament	8 × 2 127mm (5-in) DP 145 × 25mm AA 12 × 28 120mm rocket launchers
Complement	2,400 approx
Builder	Yokosuka NY
Launched	8 October 1944
Completed for passage only	19 November 1944
Sunk	29 November 1944

United Kingdom

Lack of space precludes the full story of the many changes made in the early British carriers and the reason for those changes. The details which follow apply to the state of the ships in 1939 and after.

HMS *Argus*

The first aircraft-carrying ship intended to launch and recover aircraft was completed on 19 September 1918 – less than 15 years after Orville Wright's first successful flight. This ship, HMS *Argus*, had originally been laid down in 1914 at a British yard as a fast liner, to be named *Conte Rosso* by her future Italian owners. Building was suspended at an early stage but in August 1916 the frame was purchased by the Admiralty for completion as a seaplane carrier. Before long the requirements were changed and she eventually emerged as a flush-decked aircraft carrier, the first landing being achieved in late October 1918. Between the Wars she was used extensively for trials and training and in 1938 she was modernised to operate radio-controlled target aircraft – De Havilland 'Queen Bees'.

Hull: The original passenger ship hull form was retained unmodified up to the shelter deck and the only armour was for the magazines, which had 2-in (51mm) crowns and sides. Waterline protection for the machinery was minimal, consisting of a girdle of protective plating only two inches thick. An anti-torpedo bulge was added in the 1920s, but this contributed more to the stability of the ship than to her protection, for it was intended to be proof against a charge of only 440lb (200kg) of TNT.

Machinery: The original turbines were to have driven the 15,750-ton *Conte Rosso* at a maximum speed of 19.5 knots and a cruising speed of 18 knots but the Royal Navy wanted 20.5 and 16 knots and so the commercial machinery was modified by a set of destroyer boilers which gave the desired maximum power on trials in 1918, but which were capa-

The modifications to the forward supporting structure under ARGUS *flight deck were made necessary by the addition of a hydraulic 'accelerator' in 1938. Note the chart-house in the raised position for leaving harbour.* (VIA JDB)

ARGUS – *the 'Ditty Box' – seen in the Mediterranean in 1942. Note the single lift opening, rectangular flight deck extension, elimination of cut-outs forward of lift.* (AJ WARD)

ble of giving her only 18.75 knots 21 years later. The boiler uptakes were led up to the roof of the hangar, on either side of the ship, and then ducted aft to exhaust under the after end of the flight deck, surrounded by large annular casings through which cooling air was driven by fans. The lagging and cooling system were never completely satisfactory, the smoke emerged in altogether the wrong place, under the approach path, and the position of the ducts in the 14½ft gap between the flight deck and the roof of the hangar limited the positioning of the lift to the forward third of the flight deck, so that it was hardly surprising that the lay-out was never repeated.

Flight Deck and Hangar: The flight deck was of light steel plating, supported by lattice-work over the hangar roof, which was the upper strength deck. Navigation when flying was in progress was undertaken in the bridge wings forward, on either side of the flight deck, but otherwise a retractable chart-house was raised in the centre of the deck, mounted on a hydraulic ram. By 1939, a single 'production prototype' accelerator had been installed, capable of launching an 12,000lb (5,450kg) aircraft at 66 knots 'end speed' from a trolley. By 1939, a single cruciform lift aperture with a rectangular lift platform (the 'wings' were closed off by rolling plates) connected the flight deck with the hangar deck, 34½ft below. The 20-ft high hangar had been demanded by the RAF, so that aircraft could be lifted over one another to transfer them to and from the lift and the rear entrance to the hangar – the latter opening through a steel roller door to the quarterdeck, which was the seaplane handling platform until 1938. The lift had a maximum loading of 13,440lb (6,100kg) and the four arrester wires could deal with an 11,000lb (5,000kg) aircraft landing at a relative speed of 53 knots. With the aircraft in service in 1939 this meant that about 15 knots of 'felt' wind would be needed, so that *Argus* was capable of operating all front-line aircraft in service in all wind conditions, in spite of the small size of her deck. No barrier was ever fitted. Aircraft complement on operations was usually about a dozen, but for her final front-line deployment, in late 1942, she embarked 18 non-folding Supermarine Seafire, her wide lift aperture permitting her to strike down over-large aircraft to her hangar.

Armament: In 1939, armament consisted of two 4-in (102mm) AA guns and three quadruple 0.5-in (12.7mm) AA machine guns. From 1941, 20mm Oerlikon AA guns were installed in increasing numbers and by the end of that year she had 13 Oerlikons and no 0.5s; for a short period in 1941, she carried six single 0.5-in Colt machine guns.

Career: *Argus* began and ended her War as a deck-landing training ship; in between she ferried aircraft to West Africa, Malta and North Russia and took part in convoy and assault operations in the Mediterranean. She was finally retired in late 1943, replaced in the training role by American-built escort carriers. Used as an accommodation ship until the end of the War, HMS *Argus* was scrapped in 1946.

HMS *Argus*

Displacement tonnage	
Standard	14,000
Full load	16,500
Dimensions	
Length (oa)	567ft (172.8m)
Beam (wl)	79ft 6in (24.23m)
Draught	22ft 6in (6.85m)
Flight deck	470ft (143.25m) × 85ft (25.9m) extended to 548ft in 1943 (167m)
Hangar	294ft 5in (89.7m) × 50ft (15.2m) max
Arrester wires	4
Lift	37ft 1in × 35ft 10in (11.3 × 10.9m)
Catapult	12,000lb (5,450kg) @ 66 knots (76mph = 122kph)
Aircraft stowage	12-18 (depending upon type)
Machinery	2 sets geared turbines; 2 shafts
shp	21,376 (1918 trials)
speed	18.75 knots (1939)
fuel	2,100 tons
radius	4,370nm (5,032 stm = 8,050km) at 16 knots
Aviation fuel	14,000 Imp gallons (16,800 US galls = 63,645 litres)
Armament (1943)	2 × 4-in (102mm) AA
	3 × 4 0.50-in (12.7mm) AA mg (removed 1942)
	13 × 20mm AA (11 installed 1942)
Complement	c 760
Builder:	William Beardmore, Clyde
Launched	2 December 1917
Completed	16 September 1918
Reconstructed	1937-8

HMS *Eagle*

Early in 1918, the Admiralty requisitioned the incomplete Chilean battleship *Almirante Cochrane,* whose construction on the Tyne had been suspended in 1914, by which time the hull was erected as far as the main deck. She was then completed as an aircraft carrier, the whole process taking until the autumn of 1923, although she was used for trials in 1920 to evaluate her large starboard-side island and its effect on deck-landing. When commissioned on 26 February 1924, HMS *Eagle* was the first Fleet carrier worthy of the name anywhere in the world.

Hull: As in *Argus,* the basic hull form was not altered, apart from the addition of a broad anti-torpedo bulge which was entirely underwater. The fo'c'sle deck became the strength deck and the floor of the hangar, with the 1,000 ton steel flight deck supported by steel webs forming the hangar sides and with cantilevered girders and pillars fore and aft of the hangar. The original battleship armoured belt was removed and a 4½in (114mm) waterline belt substituted to protect the machinery and magazines – the bulk aircraft fuel stowage was within this armour – and the full thickness of the 3in (76mm) armoured deck was retained over the vitals. Above this, the 1in (25mm) flight deck provided an extra layer of protection for the length of the hangar.

Flight Deck and Hangar: The ogival plan first seen in *Argus* was retained for *Eagle's* much longer and broader flight deck, there being no need to square off the deck to provide parking space forward. Unlike *Argus,* the extreme forward end was faired into the fo'c'sle by plating, to improve the airflow over the deck. Indeed, considerable attention was paid to the aerodynamics and as early as 1918 a model of the ship was tested in a wind tunnel. From these experiments emerged the characteristic cambered 'round down' to be seen in all British Fleet carriers and which smoothed out the airflow immediately behind the hull. The 130-ft long, 18-ft wide (39.6m × 5.5m) island on the starboard side encroached on the flight deck but by moving the painted deck centre-line six feet to port, sufficient space was provided for parking non-folding fighters abaft the island while still retaining a 72-ft (22m) wide clear area. Six arrester wires (of the 11,000lb/53 knot type) were fitted in 1936 but *Eagle* was never equipped with a barrier or an accelerator. A Type 72 aircraft homing beacon was fitted at the foremast-head. The forward electro-hydraulic lift was of cruciform shape and the 46 × 47-ft (14 × 14.3m) platform became standard in all subsequent conversions, while the after lift was rectangular and was only 33ft (10m) wide, being intended for folding aircraft only. Unlike all the other early British carriers, *Eagle* had no quarter-deck seaplane handling platform and the after lift was therefore plumbed by the enormous crane at the rear end of the island. Both lifts were capable of operating with a 14,000lb (6,360kg) load. Up to 18 folded Swordfish could be carried in the 20-ft high hangar, as well as four fighters in the starboard side flight deck park. Workshop space was ample, though not as luxurious as in *Argus.* Petrol stowage was in non-integral tanks with a capacity of 14,800 Imp galls (67,200 litres), increased to 17,750 galls (80,600 litres) in 1942.

Machinery: The outstanding feature of *Eagle's* machinery arrangements was the ducting of the uptakes from all four boiler-rooms horizontally across the ship below the hangar deck to the two vertical funnels on top of the island – the first aircraft carrier with the lay-out which was rapidly

EAGLE *in war-paint, 1942. Note the 'zareba' surrounding the two 4-in guns and the multiple pompom forward of the island, the radar-fitted AA director and the 'dustbin' of the Type 72 homing beacon on top of the gunnery control howdah (the Type 291 air warning radar at the mainmast head is indiscernable), the pompom between the funnels, and the two Sea Hurricanes parked clear of the landing area, immediately abaft the island.*
(LT CDR I MARTIN)

proved to be the most advantageous. The four-shaft machinery gave a trials speed of 24.37 knots in 1923, but by 1939, six years after re-boilering, *Eagle's* best speed was about 20 knots.

Armament: *Eagle* also set the gunnery style for some years to come by mounting nine 6-in (152mm) guns, for anti-destroyer protection, on the fo'c'sle and quarterdeck, with five available on each broadside. The directors for these guns were at the top of the tripod foremast, under the massive howdah which from 1933 housed the AA fire control director for the four 4-in AA guns, two mounted on the flight deck ahead of the island, one above and one below the crane abaft the island. One 8-barrelled 2-pdr pompom was located between the funnels and later a second was ahead of the two forward 4-in guns. The four quadruple 0.5-in machine guns were replaced by a dozen 20mm Oerlikons in 1942, when AA fire control radar and a short-range air and surface warning radar was fitted.

Fate: *Eagle* was hit north of Algiers by four torpedoes fired by *U-73* on 11 August 1942. Her 1918-style underwater protection was totally defeated and she sank within four minutes. There was no fire and only 158 of the crew of 951 were lost.

HMS *Eagle*

Displacement tonnage	
Standard (1933)	22,600
Full load (1942)	27,500
Dimensions	
Length (oa)	667ft 6in (203.5m)
Beam (bulges)	105ft (32m)
Draught	27ft (8.2m)
Flight deck	652ft (198.7m) × 96ft (29.3m) max
Hangar	400ft (121.9m) × 66ft (20m) max, 33ft min
Arrester wires	6
Lifts	2 – largest 46ft × 47ft (14 × 14.32m)
Aircraft stowage	(1942) 22
Machinery	4 sets geared turbines; 4 shafts
shp	52,102 (1924)
speed	c 24 knots (1940)
fuel	2,810 tons (1940)
radius	3,700nm (4,260 stm = 6,800km) at 19 knots
aviation fuel	17,750 Imp galls (21,320 US galls = 80,691 litres)
Armament (1942)	9 × 6-in (152mm) low angle
	4 × 4-in (102mm) AA
	2 × 8 2pdr (40mm) AA pompom
	12 × 20mm AA
Complement	953
Builder	Armstrong, Whitworth & Co, Tyne
Launched	8 June 1918
Completed for trials	23 April 1920
Completed (Portsmouth Dockyard)	September 1923
Commissioned	26 February 1924
Sunk	11 August 1942

HMS *Hermes*

The first ship in the world to be designed, ordered and laid down as an aircraft carrier was HMS *Hermes*. The order was placed in July 1917 and the ship was laid down in January 1918; thanks to the uncomplicated design of the basic hull, the readily available machinery and the lack of armour, she was launched in the following September. Construction was held up at the end of the War until trials with *Argus* and *Eagle,* in 1919 and 1920, had established the relative merits of the island and flush-deck lay-outs. In 1920, *Hermes* was towed to the Royal Naval Dockyard, Devonport, for completion as an island carrier, commissioning on 18 February 1924, two days before *Eagle* but five months after the latter had begun sea trials.

Hull: *Hermes* displaced over 3,000 tons less than *Argus,* being longer but narrower (even when bulged) than the converted merchantman. Her freeboard, at about 32ft (9.75m), was just over half that of *Argus* and to improve her seaworthiness the hull was plated up to the flight deck as far aft as the island, the flare of the plating tending to keep the forward end of the flight deck dry in quite heavy seas. Apart from the bulge, the only protection was a waterline thickness of up to two inches of high-tensile (not armour) steel plate and a one-inch HT flight deck.

Flight Deck and Hull: The ogive-plan flight deck was repeated, with two lifts identical to *Eagle's* forward lift at either end of the hangar. The after lift well was on the open-sided quarterdeck, originally intended as a seaplane handling area and accessible from the hangar by means of a steel-shutter door. The round-down was made more exaggerated by a hump in the flight deck, intended to form the rear anchor of the fore-and-aft arrester wire system and

HERMES *shortly before the outbreak of War, with four Swordfish on deck. One of the aircraft has just been ranged up the after lift which was located abaft the hangar, lowering into the open area forward of the quarterdeck. Note also the wind screen forward, the main-wheel and tail wheel guide lines leading to the forward lift, the marked overhang of the flight deck forward, and the lack of deck-edge AA armament.*

(MOD/CROWN COPYRIGHT)

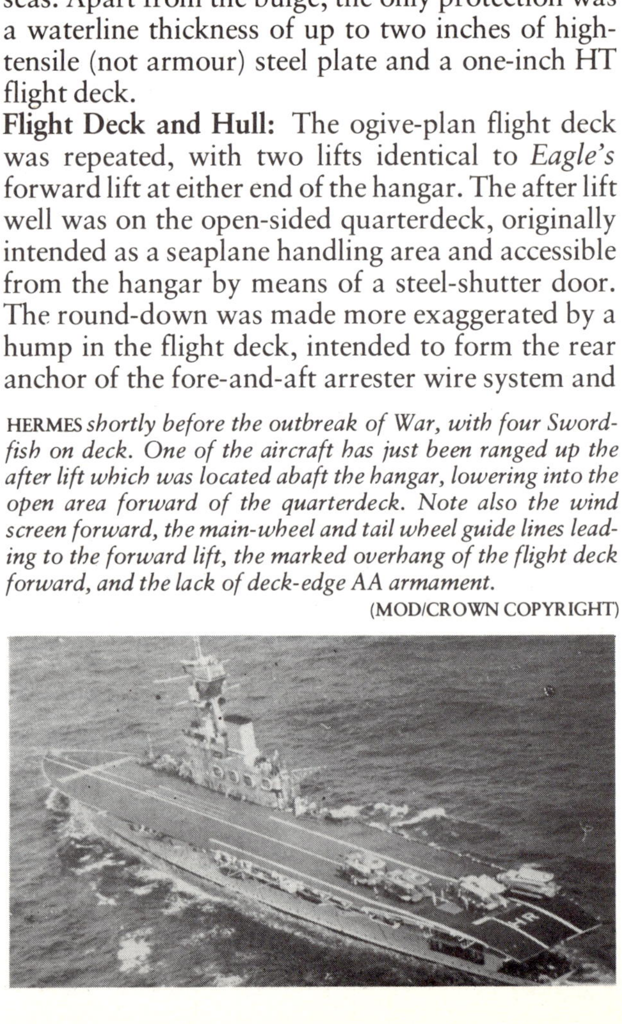

HMS HERMES, *the first ship to be designed from the outset as an aircraft carrier, seen in Chinese waters between the Wars, with a float-equipped Fairey Flycatcher under the seaplane crane.* (VIA JDB)

retained when the gear was removed in 1926; the same hump was to be seen in *Eagle* and the later *Furious* and served the secondary purpose of enabling the lift platform to be housed within the thickness of the flight deck, instead of projecting down into the hangar when raised. Four transverse arrester wires were installed as early as 1933 and were modified to stop Swordfish in 1938. The crane at the after end of the island was capable of lifting only 7,850lb (3,570kg) and was thus unable to handle a float-fitted Swordfish. The hangar was long and narrow, divided into three bays, each of which could hold only four of the 1939 torpedo-bombers – an inadequate aircraft complement for Fleet operations.

The island was disproportionately tall, having as many decks as the basic hull, but its length and width were considerably less than those of *Eagle* and the form was based on the findings of wind tunnel tests.

Machinery: The two shaft geared turbine machinery was essentially the same as that installed in the 'Flotilla Leader' destroyers launched at the same period as *Hermes*. Her speed on trials of 26.2 knots made her the fastest carrier until HMS *Furious* returned to service, but by 1939 she was capable of a speed of between 22 and 23 knots. The boiler uptakes were trunked into a single large funnel.

Armament: Like *Eagle, Hermes* was fitted with a huge gunnery control howdah above the bridge. Unfortunately, the howdah was more impressive than the armament, which consisted of three 5.5-in (140mm) low-angle guns on either beam and three 4-in AA guns, two ahead of and one abaft the island, on the flight deck. Topweight considerations prohibited a 1936 proposal to instal two twin 4-in DP mountings with an AA director. Close-range AA armament consisted of two quadruple 0.5-in machine guns and it is possible that up to half-a-dozen 20mm Oerlikons were fitted in late 1941. No radar was ever installed.

Hermes' stability was marginal by Royal Navy standards. Her bunkers could hold 2,600 tons of fuel oil, but with this load she trimmed excessively by the bow and heeled 4° to port, so that the effective maximum bunkerage was for 2,000 tons, with which her range was rather less than 4,000 miles at 18 knots. Aviation fuel capacity was also low, with only 7,500 galls available, 500 of which were carried in a jettisonable ready-use tank at the starboard side of the flight deck.

Fate: With a small aircraft complement, negligible protection and AA armament and low high-speed endurance, *Hermes* was as unfitted for operations in European waters as *Argus* and was accordingly employed for trade protection in the South Atlantic and Indian Ocean until March 1942, when she joined the Eastern Fleet. Detached to Ceylon at the beginning of April, she was found and sunk 70 miles off the coast of Ceylon on 9th; over 50 Japanese dive-bombers from carriers *Akagi, Hiryu* and *Soryu* attacked and scored hits with more than 40 250kg (551lb) semi-armour-piercing bombs. *Hermes* thus became the first (and only British) carrier to be sunk by air attack.

HMS Hermes

Displacement tonnage	
Standard	10,850
Full load	13,700
Dimensions	
Length (oa)	600ft (182.9m)
Beam (bulges)	70ft 3in (21.4m)
Draught	26ft 7in (8.1m)
Flight deck	570ft × 90ft (173.7 × 27.4m) usable
Hangar	400ft × 50ft (122m × 15m) max (approx)
Arrester wires	4
Lifts	2 – 46ft × 47ft (14m × 14.3m)
Aircraft complement	12
Machinery	2 sets geared turbines; 2 shafts
shp	42,900 (1924 trials)
speed	26.2 knots (trials)
fuel	2,000 tons (see text)
radius	2,930nm (3,375 stm = 5,400km) at 18 knots
aviation fuel	7,500 Imp galls (9,000 US galls = 34,100 litres)
Armament	6 × 5.5-in (139.7mm) low angle 3.× 4-in (102mm) AA 2 × 4 0.50-in (12.7mm) AA mg
Complement	c 700
Builder	Armstrong, Whitworth
Launched	11 September 1919
Completed	18 February 1924 (by Devonport Dockyard)
Sunk	9 April 1942

HMS *Furious*

Three ships, *Furious, Courageous* and *Glorious,* were laid down after the outbreak of the First World War as 'Large Light Cruisers', hybrid capital ships intended to operate at high speed in the shallow waters of the eastern North Sea and Baltic. *Courageous* and *Glorious,* armed with four 15-in (381mm) guns, were completed in January 1917 and saw service with the Battlecruiser Fleet; *Furious* was completed in August 1917 with an 18-in (457mm) gun aft and a flying-off deck forward. The big gun was replaced by a landing-on deck in 1918 and she was decommissioned in 1919 to await a decision as to her future. In 1922, work began on conversion to a flush-decked carrier with a superimposed second hangar deck, a short flying-off deck on to which this upper hangar opened and a seaplane handling platform over the quarterdeck abaft the lower lift. Completed in August 1925, *Furious* was thereafter modified during refits and modernisations, the last of which, in 1938-9, added a small island, closed off the forward end of the upper hangar and the after end of the lower and completely altered the main armament.

Hull: The existing superstructure and fittings were razed to the fo'c'sle deck, which became the lower hangar deck, with a two-storey box built on top for two-thirds of the ship's length. The battlecruiser-type hull had a length to beam ratio of 9.7:1, compared with the ex-battleship *Eagle's* 7:1, and to give a better range of stability, in waters other than the North Sea, bulges were added at the waterline, reducing the ratio to 8.7:1. In addition to this anti-submarine protection, *Furious* had a 3in armour belt outboard of her machinery and magazines and a 2in armoured deck over the same spaces, the whole scheme being intended to be proof against 4.7-in (120mm) gunfire and 440lb underwater charges in contact with the hull.

Flight Deck and Hangars: The flight deck was constructed of one-inch protective plating, extending from a semi-circular planform 'leading edge' nearly 200ft (60m) abaft the bows to just short of the stern, with a useful length between round-downs of 530ft. Four arrester wires were installed in 1933, the units being modernised from time to time, so that by 1944 they could handle 11,000lb aircraft landing at up to 60 knots. The lifts were identical to those in *Hermes,* with a limiting load of 12,000lb (5,450kg) and both served the two hangar decks. The hangars were of unequal length, *Furious* being unusual in that the lower hangar was longer than the upper, due to the smoke exhaust arrangements aft. Inadequate workshop space at the sides of the hangars led to part of the lower hangar being allocated for this purpose, reducing aircraft complement from a potential 46 to between 33 and 36. Specified hangar height was 16ft (4.9m), to accommodate aircraft on floats, but the minimum clear height was 15ft at both levels.

Machinery: The original four-shaft geared turbines were retained, the bulges reducing maximum speed by 1½ knots (to 30.03 knots in 1925) and old age bringing down the sea speed to 28.5 knots by 1940. The boiler uptakes were led up to the upper hangar deck level on both sides of the ship and were then ducted aft to two sets of two grilles, one pair at each side of the round-down and the other on either side of the lower hangar, the lower grilles being used when the ship was operating aircraft. The disadvantages of the system – 'wild heat' escaping and loss of hangar space – were not outweighed by the advantages expected of a flush flight deck and it was not repeated (except in the Japanese *Kaga*).

Armament: In 1939, *Furious* was re-armed with six twin 4-in DP mountings, in place of the ten 5.5-in and three 4-in AA guns which she had carried previously. One twin 4-in was mounted on what had been the flying-off deck, ahead of a fire control director which was flanked by two 8-barrelled pompoms, another was on the quarterdeck and there were two on either beam, at lower hangar

HMS FURIOUS *in the Clyde in 1942, following a refit in the USA: the twin 4-in AA guns on the fo'c'sle and quarterdeck and the two mountings on the starboard side at lower hangar deck level can be seen clearly, as can the upper edge of the anti-torpedo bulge.* (MOD/CROWN COPYRIGHT)

deck level. The island was a simple low-profile structure intended entirely for gunnery and flying control, with an AA and surface fire control director, two pompom directors and a homing beacon on a stump mast. Fore and aft of the island, on the flight deck, were two more big multiple pompoms. Two quadruple 0.5-in AA machine guns were replaced by 20mm Oerlikons, of which 15 were installed by 1943. Ranging radar was added to the directors and a lightweight air warning radar was later fitted at the front of the island. The ship was navigated from a position on the starboard deck edge during flying and from a retractable 'hut' set in the forward round-down when cruising or entering harbour.

Career: HMS *Furious* saw extensive service in the Atlantic, Arctic and Mediterranean and although often attacked never sustained a direct hit at sea. She was finally retired from operations in September 1944 and was scrapped between 1948 and 1954, following use as a target for underwater explosives trials.

'Courageous' class

The only Royal Navy capital ships ever to be designed and commissioned for operations in a limited geographical area, HMS *Courageous* and *Glorious* were of little use when WW1 came to an end. They were saved from disposal by a decision taken in 1920 to convert them as aircraft carriers along the lines of *Furious*, but work could not begin until 1925, when *Courageous* was taken in hand at Devonport, *Glorious* following two years later. Even before *Furious* was completed, the Navy had become disenchanted with ducted funnels and as the superiority of the island lay-out had already been conclusively proved, the two ships were completed with an island which contained a single large funnel. Like all earlier conversions, the class was given anti-torpedo bulges for stability – by 1939 the protective value was negligible. The armour scheme was the same as that in *Furious*.

Flight Deck and Hangars: The forward flying-off deck was discarded in 1935-36 and two accelerators were installed at the forward end of the

▲ GLORIOUS' *extended flight deck, supported by 'W'-form bracing over the raised quarterdeck, is well illustrated in this view, taken after her 1935 refit. Note also the waterline bulge, the 4.7-in AA guns on the QD, the seaplane booms over the rear opening to the hangar, the AA director on its large sponson between the raised 'hockey sticks', and the extended conning platform projecting from the port side of the island.*
(MOD/CROWN COPYRIGHT)

▼ COURAGEOUS *could be distinguished from her sister-ship from most angles but the bow by the termination of the flight deck above the quarterdeck (an awning is spread over the QD in this view, thus obscuring the position of the seaplane handling platform). The island/funnel arrangement effectively disguises the close relationship between this class and* FURIOUS.
(VIA RSD ARMOUR)

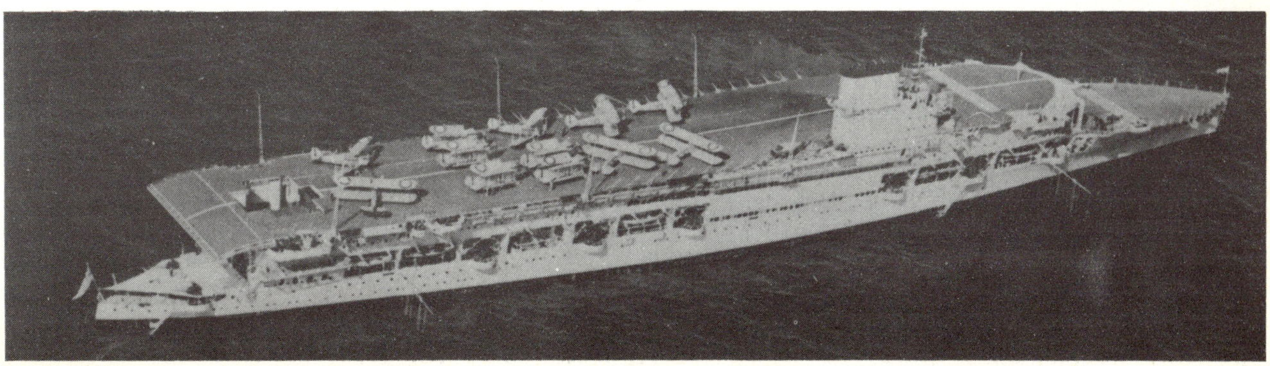

flight deck, the ends of the tracks projecting from the forward lip of the round-down. These catapults could launch an 8,000lb (3,640kg) aircraft at an end speed of 56 knots, or a 10,000lb (4,550kg) aircraft at 52 knots, and were intended primarily for floatplanes; landing back on board was no problem, for the floats fitted to British carrier-type aircraft at this period were strengthened for deck landings! *Courageous* had been the first British carrier fitted with a transverse arrester gear system, in late 1930, and since 1933 both ships had been equipped with four wires of the Mk III pattern also fitted in *Eagle, Furious* and *Hermes;* the two lifts were also of the standard 46 × 47ft type. The after ends of the two ships differed: *Courageous'* flight deck ended abruptly, with a very short round-down, at the after end of the hangar and the seaplane handling deck was built up above the quarterdeck, whereas *Glorious'* quarterdeck was on a level with the lower hangar and supported a rounded-down extension to the flight deck overhanging the stern. The upper hangar ran the full length of the 'box' and there were workshops outboard of the hangars (thanks to the lack of funnel ducting) and up to 48 aircraft could be carried with ease.

Armament: No provision was made in the class for heavy guns for use against destroyers and the 16 4.7-in (120mm) guns in single mounts forward, aft and on either beam were meant for AA use, controlled by two directors on each side, just below the flight deck. Two 8-barrelled pompoms were installed on the former forward flying-off deck and a third was located on the starboard side of the flight deck, immediately abaft the island. There were also two multiple 0.5-in machine-guns on the port deck edge.

Like *Furious,* these two ships were somewhat short-ranged, with a range of just over 2,000 miles (3,900km) at full speed, but they carried 35,700 Imp galls (162,000 litres) of petrol, compared with 22,000 galls (100,000 litres) carried by their half-sister. With a complement of 48 aircraft apiece, they would have made a considerable contribution to the war at sea had they survived the first nine months.

Fates: *Courageous* made history on 17 September 1939 by becoming the first flat-topped aircraft carrier to be sunk. As stated above, her 1922-style underwater protection was ineffective by 1939 and she succumbed in South-West Approaches to two torpedoes fired by the German *U-29.* The well-protected aviation fuel tanks were virtually full but they remained undamaged and there was no fire.

Glorious lasted until 8 June 1940, performing valuable service in the Norwegian campaign, both as an operational unit and also as a ferry carrier, taking RAF aircraft to forward airfields. When the Narvik area was evacuated, she re-embarked a number of unhooked Gladiators and Hurricane fighters by landing them on; on the next day she and her two escorting destroyers were surprised and then overwhelmed west of Narvik by the 11-in (280mm) gunfire of the battlecruisers *Scharnhorst* and *Gneisenau, Glorious'* thin armour providing no defence against such heavy metal.

HM Ships *Furious, Glorious, Courageous*

Displacement tonnage			
Standard	22,450 (*Furious*) 22,500 (others)		
Full load	27,165 (*Furious*) 27,400 (*Glorious*) 27,560 (*Courageous*)		
Dimensions			
Length (oa)	786ft 5in ± 2in (239.7m ± .05m)		
Beam (bulges)	90ft (27.4m)(*Furious*) 90ft 6in (27.6m) (others)		
Draught	28ft (8.5m)(all)		
Flight deck	576ft [530ft (161.5m) usable] × 91ft 6in (175.5m × 27.9m); *Furious'* usable deck extended to 596ft (181.6m) in 1943		
Hangars (lower)	550ft × 50ft (167.6m × 15.2m) (all)		
(upper)	520ft × 50ft (158.5m ×) (*Furious*) 550ft × 50ft (others)		
Arrester wires	4		
Catapults	2 – 8,000lb (3,640kg) @ 56 knots (64.5mph = 103kph) (not in *Furious*)		
Aircraft stowage	33 (*Furious*) 42 (others)		
Machinery	4 sets geared turbines; 4 shafts		
shp/speed	90,820/30.03 knots (1925) (*Furious*) 91,162/29.47 knots (1930) (*Glorious*) 90,670/30.5 knots (1928) (*Courageous*)		
fuel & radius	3,830 tons (*Furious*) 3,700nm (4,260 stm = 6,815km) at 20 knots 3,450 tons (*Glorious*), 3,685 tons (*Courageous*) 2,920nm at 24.5 knots		
aviation fuel	20,800 Imp galls (24,980 US galls = 94,550 litres) (*Furious*) 35,700 Imp galls (42,870 US galls = 162,300 litres) (others)		
Armament	**Furious (1942)**	**Glorious & Courageous**	
	12 × 4-in (102mm) AA 4 × 8 2pdr AA 15 × 20mm AA	12 × 4.7-in (120mm) AA 3×4 0.5-in (12.7mm)	
Complement	c 900	839	
Builder	**Furious**	**Glorious**	**Courageous**
	Armstrong, Whitworth	Harland & Wolff (Belfast)	Armstrong, Whitworth
Launched	15 August 1916	20 April 1916	5 February 1916
Completed	July 1917	June 1917	June 1917
Converted	Rosyth Dy	Devonport Dy	Devonport Dy
Completed	31 August 1925	10 March 1930	5 May 1928
Reconstructed	1938-9	—	—
Sunk	—	8 June 1940	17 September 1939

HMS *Ark Royal*

Lack of money prevented the Royal Navy from ordering a new carrier before 1935, approval having been given in the previous year. Britain was comfortably inside the carrier Treaty tonnage gross limit but had for years been campaigning for a 22,000 ton limit for individual ships, mainly for the sake of economy, and this new carrier – the first to be laid down in Britain for 17 years – was designed to this low figure.

Hull: Extensive use was made of welding in the construction of *Ark Royal,* some 65% of the structure being involved, with a saving of 500 tons. The form chosen for the hull was not particularly fine, for she had a waterline length:beam ratio of 7.6:1, but was extremely stable with considerable resistance to roll. Although she is usually referred to as 'unarmoured', this was not the case, as she had a 3.5in (89mm) lower hangar deck, covering the machinery, magazines and aviation fuel, this armour extending outboard to meet the 4.5in (114mm) side belt, the ends being enclosed by transverse bulkheads to form an inverted armoured 'box' around the ship's vitals. An improved form of bulge and an internal splinter-proof bulkhead were believed to be proof against a 750lb contact mine or torpedo.

Flight Deck and Hangars: In order to provide the largest area of flight deck on a hull whose size was limited by tonnage and docking facilities *Ark Royal's* flight deck overhung the ends of the hull, the entirety of the after round-down being over the water. Two catapults similar to those in *Argus* were installed forward, squaring-off the flight deck – all previous British carriers having had an ogival or rounded forward round-down. Eight arrester wires capable of stopping 11,000lb aircraft landing at a relative speed of 60 knots were rove to four units; a fifth unit controlled the safety barrier (the first in a British ship) which had the same entry limitations but a pull out of only 40ft (12m) instead of the 140ft (42.5m) of the wires.

The two 16ft high hangars had a total area of 52,580ft^2 (4,884m^2) – the greatest in any British carrier. Although it had been specified that the ship should accommodate and operate 72 aircraft, it was

ARK ROYAL *recovering Hawker Ospreys during her 1938 work-up; note the collapsed trolley on the port accelerator, the three lifts, the masthead Type 72 homing beacon, and the signal flag boom (horizontal) outboard of the island.*
(CHARLES E BROWN)

ARK ROYAL'S *penultimate appearance in the Home Dockyard was at Portsmouth in March 1940, when a degaussing coil (the band above the quarterdeck openings) was fitted to protect the ship against magnetically-fused underwater weapons.*
(CONWAY MARITIME PRESS)

accepted before the launch that she would carry only 60 and the scale of spares stowage, workshop capacity and ordnance was based on the lower figure. The petrol tanks were of the usual non-integral cylindrical type, with a capacity of 100,000 Imp galls (454,600 litres = 120,090 US galls) and instead of the water displacement system used since 1923, an air pressure delivery system was used to avoid contamination of the fuel by salt water.

For the first and only time, the Royal Navy opted for three lifts within the flight deck perimeter. In order to maintain the integrity of the strength deck (flight deck), the apertures were made as small as possible, two of the lifts being only 22ft (6.7m) wide, and two were offset to starboard and one to port of the flight deck centre-line. While this preserved the girder strength, it also meant that only folded or partly dismantled aircraft could be struck down or manoeuvred around the lift wells in the hangars. The lifts themselves were unconventional in that each had two platforms, the total travel of each unit being through just one deck, so that to range an aircraft to the flight deck from the lower hangar deck necessitated three separate movements of the lift – an inefficient procedure when the stated purpose of the arrangement was the speedy transfer of aircraft!

Machinery: The power to propel the ship at the specified 31 knots could not be provided by a two-shaft installation and four shafts would have led to an unacceptable increase in standard displacement; the unusual (for the Royal Navy) arrangement of three shafts and sets of machinery was therefore adopted, design output being 102,000hp. Electrical power was to have been provided by four steam-driven turbo-generators and two diesel generators, but the latter were replaced by TGs in order to give added capacity for the full 'action load' and therefore electrical power in the ship depended entirely upon steam from the boilers.

Armament: Eight twin 4.5-in (114mm) dual-purpose mountings were disposed in pairs in four batteries, near the 'corners' of the ship, each pair having its own deck-edge fire-control director. Experience was to show that the guns were mounted too high and that the benefits of being able to fire at low angles across the flight deck were outweighed by blast damage suffered by aircraft on deck. No fewer than six 8-barrelled pompoms were mounted, two forward of the island and one abaft the island on the flight deck, one on the after end of the island and two others at the port deck edge amidships. Eight quadruple 0.5-in machine-guns were also installed around the flight deck. Radar was not fitted, although by the time that she was lost all modern British carriers and most major warships had some form of warning and fire-control installation. An aircraft homing beacon was at the top of the mainmast.

Fate: After continuous service in the Atlantic, off Norway and in the Mediterranean, *Ark Royal* was at last hit east of Gibraltar on 13 November 1941. A single torpedo fired by *U-81* struck abreast the starboard wing boiler room, causing immediate flooding and a severe 'whip' of the ends of the ship; there was no fire or petrol leakage. The subsequent loss of the ship was due primarily to poor design – the underwater protection was not proof against a 750lb charge, no baffles had been built into the transverse trunking which took the smoke from the boilers across to the starboard side, there were not enough pumps and the watertight sub-division was neither adequate nor watertight. As the list increased with the ingress of water, so the water entered the uptake trunking and then the boilers themselves. When the port wing boilers were extinguished 13 hours after the torpedo hit there was no longer power to the pumps; diesel generators independent of steam supplies might have saved the ship.

HMS *Ark Royal*

Displacement tonnage	
Standard	22,000
Full load	27,720
Dimensions	
Length (oa)	800ft (243.8m)
Beam (wl)	94ft 9in (28.9m)
Draught	23ft 9in (7.2m)
Flight deck	c 720ft × 95ft (220m × 29m) usable
Hangars (upper)	568ft × 60ft (173m × 18.3m)
(lower)	452ft (137.7m) × 60ft
Arrester wires	8
Lifts	3 – largest 45 × 25ft (13.7 × 7.6m)
Catapults*	2 – 12,000lb (5,450kg) @ 66 knots (76mph = 122kph)
Aircraft stowage	60 (maximum of 54 actually operated in 1941)
Machinery	3 sets of geared turbines; 3 shafts
shp	103,000
speed	31.75 knots
fuel	4,620 tons
radius	7,620nm (8,775 stm = 14,040km) at 20 knots
Aviation fuel	100,000 Imp galls (120,090 US galls = 454,600 litres)
Armament	16 × 4.5-in (114mm) DP 6 × 8 2pdr AA 8 × 4 0.50-in (12.7mm) AA mg
Complement	1,580
Builder	Cammell, Laird & Co, Birkenhad
Laid down	16 September 1935
Launched	13 April 1937
Completed	16 November 1938
Sunk	14 November 1941

*The term 'Catapult' is used henceforward, although the official term 'Accelerator' was used by the Royal Navy throughout the War.

'Illustrious' class

In 1935, the Admiralty stated a requirement for four carriers, each with a capacity of 36 aircraft, to replace *Argus, Eagle, Hermes* and *Furious* by 1942. The deteriorating international situation accelerated the programme and the British Government approved the ordering of two carrier per year from 1937. The two ships of the first pair were *Illustrious* and *Victorious* and these were followed by a 1938 order for *Formidable* and *Indomitable,* all of which were to have a 23,000 standard displacement, an increase on *Ark Royal's* tonnage but with a 40% decrease in aircraft complement.

Hull: The new ships were shorter than *Ark Royal* but had the same waterline beam. More attention was paid to aerodynamic qualities, the forward round-down and hull plating being of more refined shape while the island and funnel were of aerofoil plan to reduce 'wake disturbance' of the airflow over the deck. The major point of interest was, of course, the armouring of these ships, which were intended to be able to continue fighting after sus-

HMS VICTORIOUS *in late 1941, still with the original long round-down.*

(MOD/CROWN COPYRIGHT)

HMS FORMIDABLE *at the end of 1942, with Supermarine Seafires parked on outriggers fore and aft of the island and an Albacore lined up for take-off. Note Type 281 air warning and control radar aerials, with the transmitter mast in the same position as* VICTORIOUS'*, the 20mm AA guns in the sponsons on either side of the round-down, and the homing beacon at the head of the foremast tripod – this was later removed in this ship and* VICTORIOUS *and replaced by an American YE beacon on a pole outboard of the funnel.*

(MOD/CROWN COPYRIGHT)

ILLUSTRIOUS *and* UNICORN *in company, summer 1943. The superficial resemblance between the two ships is plain, but the higher freeboard (with more hull openings) and apparently taller island of the Maintenance carrier are evident when the two ships are side by side. Note* ILLUSTRIOUS' *extended flight deck, the permanent deck park of 10 Seafires (three on outriggers), the combined transmitter/receiver aerial of the Type 79 radar on the foremast and the Type 281 abaft the funnel, and the six twin power-operated 20mm mountings on platforms outboard of the island.*

(MOD/CROWN COPYRIGHT)

taining damage rather than merely surviving to return to a dockyard. The hangar was made an armoured box, with a 3in flight deck extending between the lifts forming the lid, supported by six-feet deep beams, 4.5in walls and ends and a one-inch deck. The 3in horizontal armour, proof against 500lb (227kg) armour-piercing bombs or plunging 6-in (152mm) shells, was carried outside the hangar, at hangar deck level, to meet the upper edge of the 4.5in waterline belt. There was no anti-torpedo bulge but there was an internal splinter bulkhead and the standard of sub-division was superior to that of *Ark Royal.* The 5,000 tons of armour, 1,500 tons of it in the flight deck, forced a lower outline to be adopted, with freeboard reduced from 60ft (18.3m) to 38ft (11.6m), to preserve stability. The elimination of the upper hangar deck was thus inevitable.

Flight Deck and Hangar: The class was designed to operate 11,000lb aircraft with a maximum overload take-off weight of 14,000lb (6,360kg), the single catapult on the port side of the forward end of the flight deck having an end speed of 60 knots at the higher weight and the six arrester wires and two barriers being identical to those in *Ark Royal.* Three more wires were added aft in all ships and two forward wires were installed in all but *Illustrious;* at the same time, the catapult was modified to permit tail-down launches as well as trolley launches, the end speed increasing to 66 knots at 14,000lb. The overhead clearance in the hangar was the standard 16ft, but this was slightly reduced by the use of the overhead for stowage of major aircraft components; when the Vought F4U Corsair fighter became available, in 1943, their wing-tips had to be cropped to permit the wings to be folded or spread in the hangar. The lifts were the same as *Ark Royal's* two smaller lifts and proved to be capable of operating with a load of 15,000lb (6,800kg).

The standard load of 33 aircraft in *Illustrious, Formidable* and *Victorious* was increased by the adoption of outrigger stowages – U-channel beams projecting from the starboard deck edge in which the tail-wheel of the aircraft was guided and rolled outboard until the main wheels were at the edge of the deck, clear of the landing area – and a permanent deck park which had to be moved forward and aft for landing and take-off operations. This added to the burden of work of the handling parties but increased the aircraft complement to between 52 and 54 Corsairs and Grumman Avengers by March 1945. The 50,540 Imp galls of petrol carried was insufficient for high-intensity flying over a period of days and the ships were dependent upon underway replenishment from tankers in all operations undertaken in Pacific waters.

Armament: As in *Ark Royal,* the main armament consisted of 16 4.5-in DP guns, but they were mounted in 'Between Decks' countersunk turrets instead of open mountings. Three directors were mounted around the flight deck on hydraulic rams which elevated them above the level of the deck when in action* and the fourth on top of the island, whence it controlled the starboard forward battery or the entire heavy armament in barrage fire. Six multiple pompoms were disposed as in *Ark Royal* and 20mm Oerlikons were installed in increasing numbers – up to 52 in *Illustrious* by 1945; *Victorious* refitted in the USA in 1943 and was given three quadruple 40mm Bofors mountings.

Machinery: The machinery lay-out was almost identical to that in *Ark Royal,* with an increased output to compensate for the reduced fineness and increased draught. Trials were incomplete, but the specified 30.5 knots was reached by all three ships.

**Illustrious'* starboard after director was fixed in the raised position until 1943, when it was also made retractable.

'Illustrious' class

Displacement tonnage	
Standard	23,000
Full load	29,110
Dimensions	
Length (oa)	740 feet (225.5m) except *Victorious* – 745ft (227m); extended to 748ft 6in (228.1m) in 1944/5
Beam (wl)	95ft 9 in (29.2m)
Draught	29ft (8.8m)
Flight deck	620ft (189m) *Illustrious,* 670ft (204.2m) others × 95ft (29m); all extended to 740ft in 1944/45
Hangar	458ft × 62ft (139.6m × 18.9m)
Arrester wires	6-9 aft, 2 forward
Lifts	2 – 45ft × 22ft (13.7m × 6.7m)
Catapult	1 BH-III – 11,000lb (5,000kg) @ 66 knots (trolley); *Victorious* 12,500lb (5,680kg) @ 66 knots; 14,000lb (6,360kg) @ 66 knots (towed)
Aircraft stowage	33 (1941) – 54 (1945)
Machinery	3 sets geared turbines; 3 shafts
shp/speed	113,377/c 30.5 knots (*Illustrious*) 112,018/30.6 knots (*Formidable*) 111,164/c31 knots (*Victorious*)
fuel	4,850 tons
radius	8,800nm (10,130 stm = 16,200km) at 20 knots
Aviation fuel	50,540 Imp galls (60,700 US galls = 229,750 litres)
Armament (1945)	16 × 4.5-in (114mm) DP

	Illustrious	**Formidable**	**Victorious**
× 8 2pdr AA	5	6	5
× 4 40mm AA	–	–	2
× 2 40mm	–	–	2
× 1 40mm	3	–	–
× 2 20mm	19	20	23
× 1 20mm	14	14	15
Complement	1,229 (1940)	1,997 (1945)	

HMS *Indomitable*

The fourth ship ordered was to have been identical to the first, but shortly after she was laid down the design had to be modified to comply with the latest Staff Requirement – the ideal complement was 48 aircraft, not 72 or 36. By reducing the thickness of the hangar side armour to 1.5in (38mm) it was possible to raise the flight deck armour by 14ft (4.3m) without impairing stability; into this space was fitted a full-length upper hangar. The original 16ft high hangar was shortened to 168ft (51.2m) and was served only by the after lift. The 14ft over-head clearance was suitable for all existing and projected (in 1937) aircraft as British wing-folding systems were all of the rearward hingeing type – upward folding had not yet been considered.

Apart from the extra half-hangar, the most important improvement was the installation of a 33ft (10m) wide lift forward. Non-folding aircraft could now be struck down into the upper hangar, positioned obliquely and manoeuvred in the hangar on special trollies. By mid-1942, *Indomitable* was carrying 22 non-folding Sea Hurricanes, nine folding Grumman Martlets and 21 Fairey Albacores. The lack of over-head clearance in the upper hangar prevented her from carrying Corsairs and as only 22 of these fighters could have been accommodated in the lower hangar it was decided that she should operate Grumman F6F Hellcats, up to 33 being carried in the upper hangar, together with 18 Avengers divided between the two hangars.

The larger number of aircraft meant that 50% more ordnance had to be stowed, as well as a corresponding increase in petrol. The extra 25,000 Imp galls (113,600 litres) was stowed at the expense of 350 tons of furnace fuel oil; the fact that only 89 tons of petrol could be stowed in that volume gives an indication of the loss of space inherent in the British system.

The hull was five feet longer than that of *Illustrious* and *Formidable,* being the same as that of *Victorious* which, although ordered in 1937, slipped behind *Formidable* and did not complete until the spring of 1941. Armament was identical, in respect of the 4.5-in guns and pompoms but all ships differed in the number and arrangement of Oerlikons. Like her half-sisters, *Indomitable* was fitted with a variety of air warning and control radars and with gunnery ranging radars, even the pompom directors boasting a set. An important wartime modification was the lengthening of the usable flight deck, between the round-downs. This was carried out during refits, at the expense of the gentler curve of the round-down aft and involved a gain of 65ft (20m) in *Indomitable; Illustrious,* built with a very long after round-down, gained 120ft (36.5m), the overall length of the ship being increased by only 8.5ft (2.6cm) at the same time.

Careers: The four ships served in every theatre in which the Royal Navy saw action and *Victorious* even served with the US Navy in the Coral Sea. All were hit and damaged, *Illustrious, Formidable* and *Indomitable* by German dive-bombers, *Indomitable* by a German air-launched torpedo, and *Formidable* and *Victorious* by Japanese suicide aircraft; *Illustrious* sustained serious underwater damage from a near-miss suicide attack and 'Indom' took a direct hit but the aircraft and bomb bounced off the armour. The armour had been intended to be proof against 500lb armour-piercing bombs, as indeed it was, but the three ships hit by German dive-bombers sustained 1,100lb (500kg) hits on the armour and 550lb hits on the unprotected ends fore and aft of the lifts. None of these bombs penetrated to the machinery or magazines but on each of the three occasions the ship was unable to operate aircraft after the attacks. The only

INDOMITABLE *after repairs in the USA, seen in the summer of 1943. The extra depth of the second hangar can be seen in the increased height of the flight deck above the quarterdeck and the Paravane space below the port forward 4.5-in battery. US Navy-pattern AA directors are fitted and she has a Type 281 radar above the homing beacon and a Type 79 on the pole at the rear of the island.* (MOD/CROWN COPYRIGHT)

ship to sustain machinery damage via the flight deck was *Formidable* when a spall of armour was dislodged by the explosion of a suicide aircraft's bomb and passed through the hangar deck into the centre boiler room. The most serious damage sustained by any of the ships was the torpedoing of *Indomitable,* whose underwater protection was not only defeated but was itself destructive, fragments being blown in to wreck the port boiler room; the ship listed to 12½° and water entered the transverse uptake trunking, creating the situation which had led to the loss of *Ark Royal* – fortunately, the sea was calm and the pumps coped with the flooding and *Indomitable* reached harbour under her own steam.

The armoured carriers did not live up to the hopes of the Naval Staff, partly because they were designed to ward off the heaviest bombs in use with the RAF – a poor yardstick when it came to anti-shipping air striking forces. Nevertheless, in spite of the sacrifice of aircraft complement to protection, these ships were capable of carrying over 50 aircraft; by 1944, the Royal Navy was finding it increasingly difficult to man its squadrons and may not have been able to send greater numbers of aircraft to sea.

HMS *Indomitable*

Displacement tonnage	
Standard	23,000
Full load	29,730
Dimensions	
Length (oa)	745ft (227m)
Beam (w.l)	95ft 9in (29l.2m)
Draught	28ft 6in (8.7m)
Flight deck	680ft × 95ft (207.3m × 29m); extended to 745ft in 1943
Hangars (upper)	458ft × 62ft (139.6m × 18.9m)
(lower)	168ft (51.2m) × 62ft
Arrester wires	9 aft, 2 forward
Lifts	2 – largest 45ft × 33ft (13.7m × 10m)
Catapult	1 BH.III – 12,500lb (5,680kg) @ 66 knots (76mph = 122kph) (trolley; 14,000lb (6,360kg) @ 66 knots (towed)
Aircraft stowage	45 (1941) 55 (1943)
Machinery	3 sets geared turbines; 3 shafts
shp	113,253
speed	c 30.5 knots
fuel	4,500 tons
radius	8,200nm (9,440 stm = 15,100km) at 20 knots
Aviation fuel	75,400 Imp galls (90,550 US galls = 342,770 litres)
Armament	16 × 4.5-in (114mm) DP
(1942)	6 × 8 2pdr AA
	10 × 1 20mm AA
(1945)	5 × 8 2pdr AA
	2 × 4, 2 × 2 40mm AA
	21 × 2, 18 × 1 20mm AA
Complement	c 2,100 (1945)

HMS *Unicorn*

In 1938, the Admiralty ordered a unique vessel – a 'Fleet Air Army Supply and Repair Ship'. Intended to support operations by up to three 'Illustrious' class carriers, *Unicorn* was given a carrier lay-out with a starboard-side island and funnel configuration and a full length flight deck with catapult, arrester gear and barriers. Construction was delayed in 1940 by a political decision which also affected the 'Implacable' class and *Unicorn* was not completed until 12 March 1943.

Hull: In appearance, *Unicorn* resembled a foreshortened armoured Fleet carrier, carrying two hangar decks on a hull that was 100ft (30.5m) shorter but only five feet narrower. Although not intended for combat use, she was armoured, with a 2in flight deck to keep out 250lb (114kg) semi-armour-piercing bombs or 500lb medium capacity bombs, 2in crowns and 3in sides to the magazines, but no waterline belt, anti-torpedo protection consisting of a 1.4in (38mm) internal bulkhead.

Machinery: Fleet speed was not necessary and twin-shaft machinery, similar to the 'War Emergency' destroyer installation, was employed to give a trials speed of nearly 24 knots and a sea speed of 22 knots. With only two sets of machinery in nearly the same space taken up by three in the 'Illustrious' class a considerable volume was made available for extra stores and accommodation.

Flight Deck and Hangars: The forward and after round-downs were virtually eliminated in order to provide the maximum flight deck length – when completed, *Unicorn's* usable deck was only 24ft (7.3m) shorter than *Illustrious',* although the latter was just about to begin a refit during which the usable length was to be increased considerably. The single catapult was of the same pattern as that in the Fleet carriers and the six arrester wires were stressed to stop aircraft weighing up to 20,000lb (9,100kg) at speeds up to 60 knots; this Mark IV gear had first been installed in *Formidable* at the end of 1940 and was fitted in all later ships. The two lifts and cranes were also tested to 20,000lb, one of the former being of the same enlarged pattern as *Indomitable's* forward lift and the other having a width of 24ft (6.7m). The two hangars had a clear height of 16.5ft (4.7m), with an elaborate system of heavy lift and load transfer hoists and rails in the overhead, for major component removal and replacement. The after end of the upper hangar, under the round-down, was open and could be used for engine test runs; under the flight deck extension there were davits and rails for a self-propelled aircraft lighter which was stowed on the open deck abaft the hangar. The hangars were configured (and personnel carried) for the simultaneous repair of eight aircraft

HMS UNICORN *underway in the Indian Ocean in 1944, with a Grumman Avenger and two of the Swordfish which she carried for A/S protection tucked in behind the raised wind screen. The lack of 4.5-in turrets and the great freeboard compared with her length were obvious points of difference between this ship and the Fleet carriers, while* UNICORN *must have been the only modern carrier with twin island-mounted directors which overlooked the funnel.* (JDB)

with wings spread and the stowage of twelve serviceable reserve aircraft, with a full range of engine, airframe, electrical and radio workshops and spares, up to the standards of a shore-based Maintenance Unit. The total hangar area was similar to that of *Indomitable* – about 38,000ft² (3,530m²) – but the location of the lifts, in the centre of the hangar area instead of at the ends, with the inboard guide-posts obstructing the clear area, meant that only the bays forward of the forward lifts were usable by non-folding aircraft. Thus only 20 Supermarine Seafire IICs could be stowed in the hangars, but no fewer than 69 of the folding Mark III variant could be accommodated.

Armament: The main gun armament was 'four-cornered' as in the Fleet carriers, but with only one twin 4-in DP mounting in each position, controlled by two directors on the island, both forward of the funnel. Four quadruple 2-pdr pompoms were provided, two at the port deck-edge and one forward and one abaft the island, and 26 20mm Oerlikons were distributed wherever space could be found. A full range of air warning and control radars and gunnery ranging sets was fitted, as well as the standard Type 72 homing beacon.

Career: HMS *Unicorn* was pressed into operational service in 1943 as soon as she had worked-up. She was near-missed by bombs from a Focke-Wulf Fw 200 while escorting a Gibraltar convoy in June 1943. Three months later, she embarked 30 non-folding Seafires – 10 of them in a permanent deck park – for the Salerno invasion operation, during which her aircraft flew 197 sorties in four days. Thereafter, *Unicorn* was employed in her intended role, backing up the Fleet carriers from Ceylon, the Admiralty Islands and finally the Philippines. She continued in service after the War and formed part of the United Nations naval forces in the Korean War. No 'Repeat Unicorn' was ordered, in spite of the success of the design, but two of the 1942 Light Fleet class carriers were modified while building to serve as aircraft repair ships, albeit without the aircraft operating capability.

HMS *Unicorn*

Displacement tonnage	
Standard	14,750
Full load	20,300
Dimensions	
Length (oa)	646ft (197m)
Beam (wl)	90ft (27.4m)
Draught	25ft (7.6m)
Flight deck	646ft × 80ft (24.4m)
Arrester wires	6 (aft)
Lifts	2 – largest 46ft × 33ft (14m × 10m)
Catapult	1 BH III (as *Indomitable*)
Aircraft stowage	see text
Machinery	2 sets geared turbines; 2 shafts
shp	40,725
speed	23.92 knots (trials)
fuel	3,157 tons
radius	7.550nm (8,700 stm = 13,900km) at 20 knots
Aviation fuel	36,000 Imp galls (43,230 US galls = 163,656 litres)
Armament	8 × 4-in (102mm) AA
	4 × 4 2pdr AA
	10 × 2, 6 × 1 20mm AA
Complement	c 1,200
Builder	Harland & Wolff (Belfast)
Laid down	29 June 1939
Launched	20 November 1941
Completed	12 March 1943

'Implacable' class

The Naval staff issued a revised requirement for the Fleet carrier ordered in 1938, demanding a speed of at least 32 knots, and 35 knots if possible, a complement of 54 aircraft, but no increase in the 23,000 tons standard displacement. By the time that the second unit of the class was ordered in 1939 there had been second thoughts as to the thickness of *Indomitable's* hangar walls and a slight increase was demanded, again without any increase in displacement or reduction in stability.

Hull: The two new ships, *Indefatigable* and *Implacable,* were 26ft (8m) longer than *Illustrious* but had the same beam, being subject to the same docking limitations. A four-shaft machinery lay-out was shoe-horned into the width used by three sets of turbines and boilers in *Illustrious,* the main external difference in appearances being the considerably larger funnel.

Armour was similar to that in *Indomitable,* except that the hangar walls were of 2in thickness and the lower hangar deck was between 1.5 and 2.5in (38-63mm) thick, the heavier gauge being over the machinery as the magazines were given separate 2-3in crowns. The scheme was now superior to that of *Illustrious,* apart from the thinner hangar walls, although the total weight of armour was 1,300 tons less. The sacrifice made for the extra half-inch on the hangar walls was in the height of the lower hangar, reduced to 14ft – the same as the upper hangar. Freeboard at the flight deck was 50ft (15.2m), only 12ft more than *Illustrious* and 2ft less than *Indomitable.*

Flight Deck and Hangars: The lifts, three barriers and 11 arrester wires (two forward) were all designed to accommodate 20,000lb aircraft, the forward lift being of the 45 × 33ft (13.7 × 10m) type, serving only the forward hangar. The single H-III catapult on the port side forward was of the

INDEFATIGABLE *before initial flying trials early in 1944. No AA director is yet fitted on the after end of the island, to which it was removed from the port after deck edge, but the 'bowl' of the Type 277 height-finder can be seen forward of the foremast, in place of the director featured in the earlier armoured carriers and shifted to the flight deck forward of the island in this class. Note also the single multiple pompom bandstand abaft the island, the gallery of single 20mm guns under the round-down, the tiers of single and twin 20mm guns on the starboard side of the island, and the absence of the Type 79 at the foremast head.* ▲ (MOD/CROWN COPYRIGHT)

IMPLACABLE'S *most apparent external difference from her sister-ship was the location of her island-mounted AA director, forward of the after tripod –* INDEFATIGABLE'S *was on the extreme after end of the island. The two 'towers' forward of the island are radar-equipped pompom directors and the short lattice mast immediately ahead of the foremost 'hockey-stick' bears the VHF R/T direction-finder aerial.* ▼ (MOD/CROWN COPYRIGHT)

same basic design as that in the earlier armoured carriers but was able to launch heavier loads × 20,000lb at 56 knots and lesser loads at up to 66 knots (76mph = 122km/h) – using a trolley running in two tracks instead of one. The elimination of the one-ton trolley for launching American-built aircraft by the tail-down method gave a 4knot increase in end-speed, subject to the absolute maximum of 66 knots.

The low overhead clearance in the lengthened lower hangar did not allow the stowage of floatplanes or even the Supermarine Walrus amphibian; more important, these ships were unable to stow Corsairs in the hangars and the non-availability of Hellcats obliged the Royal Navy to embark Seafires, 48 of these short-ranged interceptors being carried in addition to 12 Fairey Fireflies and 21 Avengers. *Implacable* needed a vast deck park with this complement, for her Air Engineering Department used the lower hangar as a workshop area. The specified aircraft complement was thus handsomely exceeded, but at the cost of 'flying endurance', for the 94,650 Imp galls (430,000 litres) of aviation fuel were sufficient for only five sorties for each aircraft embarked.

Machinery: As mentioned above, a four-shaft installation was fitted into this class, the total output increasing to 152,000hp to give a maximum speed on trials of 32.3 knots; at the normal maximum full power, a sea speed of 31 knots could be maintained with ease.

Armament: The eight twin 4.5-in DP turrets were located outboard of the lifts, as in the previous armoured carriers, with three directors on the starboard side (fore, aft and on the island) capable of bearing on either beam, and one below the port deck edge. The six pompoms were also redistributed, with one being moved from the rear end of the island to the port side. A few single 40mm Bofors were added in 1945, taking the place of some of the 60-odd Oerlikons. The usual warning, gunranging and control radars were fitted, as well as the homing beacon.

Careers: *Indefatigable,* ordered in 1939, was completed on 3 May 1944 and undertook her first operation 17 days before *Implacable* was completed on 28 August 1944. Both ships served with the Home Fleet and then the British Pacific Fleet. On 1 April 1945, *Indefatigable* achieved the dubious distinction of becoming the first British carrier to be struck by a *Kamikaze,* sustaining a direct hit at the base of the island; some 'offices' were wrecked and a barrier rendered unusable, but she was fully operational within 30 minutes. *Implacable* was never attacked, arriving in the Pacific too late to take part in the hectic Okinawa campaign.

'Implacable' class

Displacement tonnage		
Standard	23,450	
Full load	32,110	
Dimensions		
Length (oa)	766ft 5in (233.6m)	
Beam (wl)	95ft 9in (29.2m)	
Draught	29ft 4in (8.9m)	
Flight deck	760ft × 90ft (231.6m × 27.4m)	
Hangars (upper)	458ft × 62ft (139.6m × 18.9)	
(lower)	208ft (63.4m) × 62ft	
Arrester wires	9 aft, 3 forward	
Lifts	2 (as *Indomitable*)	
Catapult	1 BH III (twin track) – 20,000lb (9,090kg) @ 56 knots (64.5mph = 103kph) or, 16,000lb (7,270kg) @ 66 knots (towed)	
Machinery	4 sets geared turbines; 4 shafts	
	Implacable	**Indefatigable**
shp	151,200	150,935
speed	31.89 knots	32.06 knots
fuel	4,690 tons	4,810 tons
radius @ 20 knots	6,720nm (7,738 stm = 12,380km)	6,900nm (7,945 stm = 12,710km)
Aviation fuel	94,650 Imp galls (113,660 US galls = 430,300 litres)	
Armament	16 × 4.5in (114mm) DP	
× 8 2pdr AA	5	5
× 4 2pdr	3	1
× 2 20mm	21	19
× 1 20mm	19	17
Complement	c 2,300	

Armoured Fleet Carriers	**Builder**	**Building Time** (months)	**Completed**
Illustrious	Vickers, Armstrong (Barrow)	37	25 May 1940
Formidable	Harland & Wolff (Belfast)	41	24 November 1940
Victorious	Vickers, Armstrong (Tyne)	48	15 May 1941
Indomitable	Vickers, Armstrong (Barrow)	37	10 October 1941
Indefatigable	John Brown (Clyde)	54	3 May 1944
Implacable	Fairfield (Clyde)	62	28 August 1944
Light Fleet Carriers			
Colossus	Vickers, Armstrong (Tyne)	30½	16 December 1944
Vengeance	Swan, Hunter (Tyne)	26	15 January 1945
Venerable	Cammell, Laird (Birkenhead)	25½	17 January 1945
Glory	Harland & Wolff (Belfast)	31	2 April 1945
Ocean	A Stephens & Sons (Clyde)	33	8 August 1945

Triumph, Theseus, Warrior of this class completed post-War. *Perseus, Pioneer* completed 1945 as Maintenance Carriers

'Colossus' class

Two completely new carrier designs were approved in the spring of 1942, one for a 37,000-ton armoured ship capable of operating 100 aircraft and the other a 13,190-ton 'utility carrier' with a complement of 24 aircraft. None of the four ships of the former type was launched before the end of the war and it was not until 1951 and 1955 that *Eagle* and *Ark Royal* were completed, the other two ships being cancelled at the end of the war. The 'Light Fleets' were built in quantity, ten hulls of the 1942 design and six of the 1942 (Modified) design being laid down by the end of 1943, and of these five carriers and two Aircraft Repair Ships were in commission by 15 August 1945.

Hull: The Light Fleets were built to mercantile hull standards – this has often been taken to mean that they were intended for post-war conversion as merchant ships but in fact this formula embraced only the structural strength and the nature of the internal sub-division; designed from the keel up as carriers, the between-decks arrangements below the hangar deck and the warship machinery would have been totally unsuitable for any imaginable commercial use and the cost of reconstruction would have been prohibitive.

Economy was effected by the total omission of armour protection, with the exception of mantlets (armoured caps) for 32 torpedo warheads; magazines and machinery were protected only by thin (10mm) anti-splinter bulkheads and buoyant drums. The watertight subdivision depended upon the integrity of transverse bulkheads, the only major longitudinal compartmentation being in the machinery spaces, where the two boiler-rooms and two engine rooms were staggered in *échelon* and steam pipes were so arranged that the port boilers could provide steam to the starboard turbines and the starboard boilers could supply the port turbines in the event of damage. Elsewhere in the hull, a single torpedo hit would result in the flooding of at most two complete sections and the flooding would be from side to side, avoiding large initial angles of heel.

Machinery: Experience up to 1942 had shown that the Fleet carriers had seldom needed to exceed 25 knots and this speed was therefore specified for the Light Fleets. The installation employed for *Unicorn* was repeated, the lighter and finer carriers making about a knot more on trials on the same power.

Flight Deck and Hangar: Although displacing 10,000 tons less than the 'Illustrious' class, the Light Fleets were only 53ft (16m) shorter and 16ft narrower than the armoured ships which they resembled. They thus sacrificed little in the way of flight deck and hangar area and because they carried no flight deck armour the single hangar had a clear overhead height of 17.5ft (5.3m). Intended to operate 14,000lb aircraft, they were equipped with a single BH-III twin-track catapult and five Mark VII arrester units controlling eight wires and two barriers, the wires being able to stop aircraft of up to 15,000lb weight at up to 60 knots. The two lifts were of a new type, first fitted in the escort carrier HMS *Pretoria Castle* in 1943, measured 45 × 34ft (13.7 × 10.4m), and also had a weight limitation of 15,000lb. The hangar was shorter and narrower than *Illustrious'*, but a bay was provided forward of the forward lift to accommodate two unfolded aircraft undergoing major overhaul and there was a total of 2,450ft^2 (227m^2) workshop area around the hangar. Although designed for 24 1942-size aircraft, the Light Fleets proved to be capable of operating up to 21 Corsairs and 18 Fairey Bar-

The small funnel and unencumbered slab sides fore and aft permit no confusion between the Light Fleet GLORY *and any of the preceding classes of British carriers. As completed, she was equipped with both main types of air warning and control radar – Type 79 and 281, Type 277 height-finder on top of the island and YE homing beacon on a pole above the tripod, as well as VHF D/F between the forward starboard side gun sponsons. The FG-1D Corsairs were retained until 1946, but the original Fairey Barracuda dive-bombers were replaced by Fireflies shortly after the War.* (VIA R PRIESTLY-COOPER)

racudas – the standard load for the four ships which arrived in the Far East shortly before the end of the War.

Armament: For the first time, the main defensive armament of the carrier was recognized to be her aircraft and long-range AA guns were not mounted, with a saving of over 800 tons weight compared with the armoured carriers. The initial outfit consisted of six quadruple pompoms and 19 20mm mountings – the number of twins and singles varying from ship to ship. Two ships, *Venerable* and *Vengeance,* exchanged eight twin Oerlikons for single Bofors at Sydney in July 1945, the heavier guns being needed to stop suicide aircraft. A full outfit of air warning, control and height-finding radars was installed and the pompom directors were equipped with radar ranging; the US Navy's 'YE' homing beacon, smaller and more powerful than the Type 72, was provided.

The simplicity and austerity of the design resulted in some remarkable building times, notably by Cammell, Laird Ltd, of Birkenhead, who laid down *Venerable* on 3 December 1942 and handed her over on 17 January 1945. Their simple machinery and light armament required fewer personnel than the armoured ships and this, combined with their low running costs, made them particularly attractive ships for peace-time retention and they formed the backbone of the post-war British Commonwealth Fleet.

'Colossus' class

Displacement tonnage			
Standard	13,190		
Full load	18,040		
Dimensions			
Length (oa)	693ft 2in-695ft (211.3-211.8m)		
Beam (wl)	80ft-80ft 4in (24.38-24.48m)		
Draught	23ft 5in (7.1m)		
Flight deck	690 × 80ft (210 × 24.4m)		
Hangar	445ft × 52ft (135.6 × 15.8m)		
Arrester wires	8 (all aft)		
Lifts	2 – 45ft × 34ft (13.7 × 10.4m)		
Catapult	1 BH III (twin track) – as *Indefatigable*		
Aircraft stowage	37		
Machinery	2 sets geared turbines; 2 shafts		
shp	39,775-40,339 (trials)		
speed	23.5-24.5 (trials)		
fuel	3,167-3,196 tons		
radius	7,350nm (8,460 stm = 13,540km) at 20 knots		
Aviation fuel	98,600 Imp galls (118,400 US galls = 448,230 litres)		
Armament (August 1945)	6 × 4 2pdr AA (all ships)		
	First Three	*Glory*	*Ocean*
× 1 2pdr	—	—	7
× 1 40mm	21	—	12
× 2 20mm	—	11	—
× 1 20mm	—	10	—
Complement	c 1,300		

United States

USS *Langley*

The US Congress approved the conversion of a Fleet auxiliary to an aircraft carrier in 1919. The collier *Jupiter* (AC.3) was selected and work began in the following year. Re-named *Langley,* she was also redesignated 'CV.1' – 'Cruiser, Heavier-than-Air Craft No 1' – indicating that she was regarded as a combatant unit, rather than an auxiliary like the first seaplane carrier, USS *Wright* (AV.1). Commissioned on 20 March 1922, the first take-off and landing occurred in October, Lieutenant Commander G de C Chevalier becoming the second American to land aboard a ship, over ten years after Eugene Ely.

Langley, known as the 'Covered Wagon' from her high-sided blunt-ended appearance and stately rather than rapid progress, was the only American carrier for five years and in that period she was used to develop operating techniques and Fleet aircraft tactics. Joned by *Lexington* and *Saratoga* in 1928, she remained part of the Fleet until September 1936, when she began a third career, this time as a Seaplane Carrier (AV.3). The after two-thirds of the flight deck was retained, together with half the hangar, but the remainder of the structure was cut away between the forecastle and the hangar to provide a handling deck. By the outbreak of the war in the Pacific, she was serving in yet another role, that of Aircraft Transport, and it was while ferrying USAAF fighters to Java that *Langley* was found and sunk by Japanese Naval Air Force land-based long-range bombers, on 27 February 1942.

Hull and Machinery: The collier hull and machinery were unaltered. The complicated coaling gantries were removed and the hangar built on the original upper deck; between decks extra accommodation was built in and aviation stores and workshops provided. The single funnel was replaced by two hinged smoke stacks on the *port* side, lying horizontal during flying and raised to a near vertical position when cruising. The machinery was of the turbo-electric drive type favoured by the US Navy, with the turbines driving generators which in turn supplied electric motors to drive the propellers. Long propeller shafting, often a vulnerable feature, was thus eliminated and improved response to demands for speed changes was obtained. *Langley's* main shortcoming, apart from her small size, was her low speed, for she could attain only 14 knots in service – adequate for the first generation of carrier aircraft but insufficient by the mid-'30s.

Flight Deck and Hangar: The wooden flight deck was of rectangular plan-form, unlike the ogive seen in British carrier or *Hosho's* 'pear'-shaped plan. Extending from just abaft the bows to the stern, the deck was supported by a framework of webs, beams and girders as a relatively light superstructure, the strength deck being the hangar deck. Apertures were left in the sides of the hangars, with one large 'hole' on either side for recovering seaplanes. Initially, seaplane launches were made from one of the two pneumatic catapults set in the flight deck, but seaplanes were seldom used and the 6,000lb/40 knots gear was removed in 1928 as it was not needed for wheeled aircraft launches. A 'belts and braces' arrangement of longitudinal and transverse arrester gear was used at first, but the fore-and-aft wires were soon removed. The hangar sides were not plated over as it had been found that the benefits of improved hangar ventilation outweighed the lack of complete 'weather-tightness'. A single lift interconnected hangar and flight deck and as it did not break any strength deck it could be of large dimensions. In spite of her small size, *Langley* carried and operated up to 30 aircraft.

USS *Langley*

Displacement tonnage	
Standard	11,500
Full load	c 14,700
Dimensions	
Length (oa)	542ft (165.2m)
Beam (wl)	65ft 6in (19.96m)
Draught	24ft (7.3m)
Flight deck	534ft × 64ft (162.7m × 19.5m)
Arrester wires	6?
Catapults	2 (1922-28) – 6,000lb (2,730kg) @ 40 knots (46mph = 74kph)
Lift	1
Aircraft stowage	up to 33, using 'hold' below hangar for reserve aircraft
Machinery	set generating turbine – electric motors driving 1 shaft
shp	7,150
speed	14 knots (service)
fuel	2,300 tons
radius	12,260nm (14,117 stm = 22,600km) at 10 knots
Aviation fuel	134,000 Imp galls (162,000 US galls = 612,000 litres)
Armament	4 × 5-in (127mm) low-angle AA machine guns
Builder	Mare Island Navy Yard, Cal.
Launched (as collier)	24 August 1912
Reconstructed	March 1920-July 1922
(Commissioned	20 March 1922)
Sunk	27 February 1942

'Saratoga' class

Even before the signature of the Washington Treaty, the US Navy had drawn up provisional plans for the completion of two hulls under construction as aircraft carriers. *Lexington* and *Saratoga* had been laid down as 33,500-ton, 33-knot battlecruisers to rival the Royal Navy's 'Hood' class and Japanese 'Amagi' class; the Treaty was intended to halt any such escalatory programmes and indeed only HMS *Hood* was completed as a battlecruiser, the two American ships and the Japanese *Akagi* being converted while building to carriers. Although the agreed maximum standard displacement for an individual carrier was set at 33,000 tons, two such ships being allowed to each Navy, a special clause permitted an additional 3,000 tons for horizontal protection against bombs. The US Navy took full advantage of this clause, so that while the standard displacement was always quoted as being 33,000 tons, it was in fact nearer 36,000 tons.

Hull: The battlecruiser hull form was preserved up to the level of the original fo'c'sle deck, which became the hangar deck. The steel flight deck was the strength deck – an unusual arrangement in American carriers and one which was not repeated for many years – and it was faired into the hull at bow and stern by steel plating, with round-downs fore and aft. The armoured belt was greatly reduced in thickness, but there were still 6in (152mm) at the waterline; horizontal protection consisted of a one-inch hangar deck and two inches on the lower deck over magazines and machinery. As in all US Navy carriers, the aviation fuel was carried in integral bulk tanks, surrounded by voids which could be filled with inert carbon dioxide gas.

Flight Deck and Hangar: The 888ft long (270m) flight deck was unsurpassed for sheer size for 18 years and all 90 aircraft that could be carried in 1930 could be ranged at the same time for take-off. The steel flight deck was sheathed with wood planking, suitably fire-proofed, which provided a virtually non-skid surface for aircraft handling and taxying. A single inertia-type (electrically-driven flywheel) catapult was set in the deck to starboard of the centre-line but was removed in about 1931. At the same time, a safety barrier was added, abreast the island. Two large lifts, one by the island and the other abaft the funnel, connected the flight deck with the vast single hangar deck. The hangar was not 'open' in the usual American sense, with large apertures that could be closed by shutters, but it was open to the outside air in way of the boat decks to improve natural ventilation. Although vast, the hangar could not accommodate all the aircraft that could be operated (90 as completed, 88 in 1942 and

LEXINGTON *seen on 8 May 1942, after the torpedo hits which had increased her draught forward by several feet and not long before the petrol explosion which led to her loss. Note the CXAM radar mounted at the forward end of the funnel, the 20mm AA guns on the funnel platforms and the 2 Deck sponson, and the absence of 8-in turrets.* (US NAVY)

69 in 1944) and the US Navy therefore adopted the use of a permanent deck park at a very early stage. Eight transverse arrester wires were controlled by hydraulic units from 1931, the previous system having consisted of anchored longitudinal wires and weighted transverse wires.

Machinery: The four-shaft turbo-electric machinery was the most powerful in any warship built prior to 1939 and gave a maximum trials speed of 34 knots. The uptakes from the 12 boilers were routed to the starboard side into a single enormous vertical funnel, located separate from and abaft the island. The electric generating power of the turbines was such that USS *Lexington* supplied the city of Tacoma with 4¼ million kilowatt-hours between 17 December 1929 and 16 January 1930 when the city's power station broke down.

Armament: Like the Imperial Japanese Navy, the US Navy took full advantage of the clause permitting the mounting of 8-in (203mm) guns. Two twin turrets were installed forward of the island, which was primarily a gunnery control and navigating feature, and two abaft the funnel, on which the searchlights were mounted. Twelve single open 5-in (127mm) AA guns were installed in sponsons around the deck edge. In early 1942, the 8-in turrets were removed from the two carriers; in *Saratoga,* they were replaced by four twin 5-in DP turrets and four of the deck-edge single 5-in guns were removed, but as no DP turrets were available for *Lexington,* she therefore shipped four of the most useless automatic AA weapons of the War – the quadruple 1.1-in (28mm) 'machine-gun' and was lost before she could be properly re-armed. *Saratoga's* close-range AA armament was continually improved and by 1945 she was armed with 96 40mm Bofors and 24 20mm Oerlikons, as well as the 16 5-in guns. Both ships were fitted with 'YE' aircraft homing beacons and 'CXAM' radar before the War, the radar being fitted on a bracket at the forward end of the funnel, and from 1942 *Saratoga* possessed two radar-equipped AA control directors, one on top of the island and the second on a sponson on the after end of the funnel.

Fates: *Lexington* was hit by two torpedoes and two light bombs in the Coral Sea on 8 May 1942. The 'whip' induced by the torpedoes and the mining

SARATOGA *in Puget Sound, six days after the loss of* LEXINGTON. *The 8-in turrets have been replaced by twin 5-in/38-calibre DP turrets, controlled by radar-equipped directors on top of the island and mounted on the after end of the funnel. The island has been enlarged and a light pole mast has taken the place of the original tripod; CXAM warning and control radar is installed on the forward end of the funnel. The 20mm Oerlikons outboard of the funnel are mounted in individual bandstands, instead of in a long gallery, as in* LEXINGTON. (US NAVY)

effect of many near miss bombs distorted the hull and ruptured the petrol tanks and the surrounding bulkheads. The inflammable vapour quickly spread through the ship and was detonated an hour after the attack, starting uncontrollable fires which touched off a second major explosion two hours later. She was abandoned when the fire reached her magazines and was finally scuttled by destroyer torpedoes.

Saratoga was damaged by Japanese submarine torpedoes on 11 January and 31 August 1942, sustaining widespread flooding on each occasion. She was severely damaged by a *Kamikaze* on 21 February 1945, sustaining 315 casualties. A target ship at Bikini in 1946, she sank on 25 July 1946, a few days after the first explosion, due to gradual flooding.

'Saratoga' class

Displacement tonnage		
Standard	36,000	
Full load	47,700	
Dimensions		
Length (oa)	888ft (270.7m); 901ft (274.6m) in 1944	
Beam (wl)	105ft 6in (32m)	
Draught	32ft (9.75m)	
Flight deck	880ft × 90ft (266.7m × 27.4m); 895ft (272.8m) from 1944	
Arrester wires	8	
Lifts	2	
Catapults	2 H-IVC from 1942: 16,000lb (7,270kg) @ 74 knots (85mph = 136kph) *(Saratoga only)*	
Aircraft stowage	88 (1942)	
Machinery	4 sets generating turbines – 2 electric motors on each of 4 shafts	
shp	180,000 (210,000hp on trials)	
speed	*Lexington* 34.24 knots *Saratoga* 33.91 knots	
fuel	9,748 tons	
radius	6,960nm (8,015 stm = 12,820km) at 20 knots	
Aviation fuel	110,140 Imp galls (132,264 US galls = 500,700 litres)	
Armament	**Lexington (1941)**	**Saratoga** (1944)
	8×5-in (127mm) AA	8 × 5-in DP, 8×5-in AA
	6×4 1.1-in (27.94mm) AA	23×4, 2×2 40mm
	c 30×20mm AA	12×2 20mm AA
Complement	**Saratoga** (1944) 2,381	
	Lexington (CV.2)	**Saratoga** (CV.3)
Builder	Fore River Sb (Quincy)	New York Sb
Launched	3 October 1925	7 April 1925
Commissioned	14 December 1927	16 November 1927
Sunk	8 May 1942	

USS *Ranger*

With 69,000 tons left for carrier construction after the conversion of *Saratoga* and *Lexington,* the US Navy decided to order five 13,800-ton ships, each with a capacity of 76 aircraft. Congressional approval was obtained for one such carrier in 1930, after a Committee had examined the Navy's proposals and questioned the usefulness of such a relatively light ship. Laid down in September 1931, *Ranger* (CV.4) was the first purpose-built American carrier and owed more to the lay-out of *Langley* than to the 'Saratoga' class. Completed in June 1934, a year after *Ryujo,* the only equivalent Japanese or British design, she was overweight at 14,500 tons standard and proved to be unsuitable for Pacific combat operations when the United States entered the war.

Hull: *Ranger* was built with a long, relatively narrow hull to take full advantage of her low horsepower in order to reach the specified 29.5 knots maximum speed. Armour protection was limited to a 2in (51mm) waterline belt and a 1in hangar deck, which was also the strength deck. Internal subdivision was not on the same scale as that in contemporary warships of other types.

Flight Deck and Hangar: Originally conceived as a flush-decked carrier, it was decided to add a starboard-side island while the ship was actually under construction, experience with the 'Saratoga' class having demonstrated the advantages. The wood-sheathed flight deck was less than the full length of the ship when completed, but during the war the forward end was extended to the bows. No catapult was fitted initially; the increase in aircraft weights and take-off speeds in the late '30s resulted in a change of policy in the fitting of catapults and *Ranger* was equipped with two H-II units, launching 7,000lb (3,120kg) aircraft at 61 knots. Six arrester wires and a barrier were installed and there were two large lifts, dividing the hangar into three bays. The single hangar deck had four large side apertures to port and three to starboard, closed by light steel shutters when necessary and with clear dimensions of approximately 50 × 18ft (15 × 5.5m). Two of the openings on each side were overhung by cranes mounted by supporting pillars; the cranes served to embark and disembark aircraft and also to handle the ship's launches, usually stowed in the hangar. All 76 of the 1934-vintage aircraft could be carried in the hangar, and by employing a deck-park *Ranger* was able to operate 72 Grumman Wildcats and Douglas Dauntlesses in 1942.

Machinery: Surprisingly for a ship of her size, *Ranger* had only two shafts, the machinery being half of that installed in the contemporary 'Northampton' class heavy cruisers. Each of the six boilers

USS RANGER, *the US Navy's first 'custom-built carrier', seen passing Manhattan Island during her first commission, in 1934. Note the small radius of curvature of the after ramp, the funnel hingeing arrangements, the cranes mounted at the extremities of the hangar side openings, and the short-barrelled 5-in AA guns.* (US NAVY)

had its own uptake to a hinged funnel, there being three funnels on either side of the hangar deck, right aft. During flying operations, all six funnels hinged down to the horizontal but at other times they were raised to the near-vertical, with the tops of the stacks some 15ft above flight deck level. The boilers were installed adjacent to the funnels to reduce the length of the uptakes.

Armament: Just as armour had been sacrificed to save weight, so also was the gun armament limited to just eight single 5-in AA mountings, disposed in pairs on either side of the gallery deck, fore and aft, controlled by two directors on the island. Quadruple 1.1-in AA guns were added in 1940, but these were removed, and by 1944 the close-range armament consisted of 24 40mm and 46 20mm AA guns.

USS *Ranger*

Displacement tonnage	
Standard	14,500
Full load	c 20,500
Dimensions	
Length (oa)	769ft (234.4m)
Beam (wl)	80ft (24.4m)
Draught	19ft 9in (6m)
Flight deck	c 750ft × 80ft (228.6m × 24.4m) (1943)
Hangar	c 500ft × 70ft (152m × 21m)
Arrester wires	6
Lifts	2
Catapults	2 H-II from 1942: 7,000lb (3,120kg) @ 61 knots (70mph = 112kph)
Machinery	2 sets geared turbines; 2 shafts
shp	53,500 (trials – 58,700)
speed	29.5 knots (trials – 30.35 knots)
fuel	3,100 tons
radius	9,960nm (11,470 stm = 18,350km) at 15 knots
Aviation fuel	130,500 Imp galls (156,734 US galls = 593,300 litres)
Armament (1943)	24 × 40mm AA
	46 × 20mm AA
Complement	c 2,000
Builder	Newport News Sb
Laid down	26 September 1931
Launched	25 February 1933
Commissioned	4 June 1934

'Yorktown' class

Even before *Ranger* was launched, the US Navy had revised its assessment of the ideal tonnage for a carrier, principally because it was realised that CV.4 would be too slow, ill-protected and under-armed. CV.5 and 6, *Yorktown* and *Enterprise*, were authorised in 1933 as 19,800-ton, 33-knot ships with a capacity of over 80 aircraft. Their lay-out reflected all the experience gained by the US Navy in aircraft carrier operations since 1922 and their design became the basis of the subsequent 'Essex' class. A third 'Yorktown' class carrier, *Hornet* (CV.8), was authorised in 1938 in response to Japanese naval expansion; the decision to use the five-year-old design was fully justified by the reduced building time, *Hornet* commissioning only 25 months after she had been laid down.

Hull: Like *Ranger*, the 'Yorktown' class ships possessed a very high hull:beam ratio (over 9:1) but in spite of a flight-deck freeboard of 55ft (16.8m) they were extremely stable. This was due in part to the distribution of armour, consisting of a 4in waterline belt and a total thickness of three inches of deck armour divided between the hangar deck and the main armoured deck which met the top of the belt armour. The scheme was intended primarily for protection against shell-fire and bombs, extensive sub-division being intended to cope with underwater weapons by containing, rather than preventing flooding.

Flight Deck and Hangar: The wooden flight deck terminated short of the bows but overhung the stern with only the suggestion of an after round-down. As in *Ranger*, the deck was a relatively light superstructure, supported by pillars and girders over a cavernous open-sided hangar. Two H-I catapults were installed at the bows of the flight deck–designed for the class, they could launch a 5,500lb (2,500kg) aircraft at 40 knots. A third H-I, capable of launching in either direction, was installed in the hangar, aligned with apertures to port and starboard – a latter-day equivalent of the British and Japanese lower flying-off decks. The hangar catapult was seldom used and was removed from *Enterprise* in 1943, when she was refitted with two H-IV deck catapults. Nine arrester wires were installed aft and four forward, together with four barriers; with the 1½-in wires originally installed, aircraft weight on entry was only 8,400lb (3,820kg) maximum but with thicker wires and modified units, *Enterprise* was later able to operate aircraft of up to 15,000lb (6,820kg). Three large lifts, the midships one off-set to port, served the hangar; the after lift was fitted with a turntable which simplified the task of the handling parties by eliminating the need for precise alignment when spotting the aircraft on the platform. In December 1941, the standard load was 72 aircraft; *Hornet* managed to carry and launch 16 31,000lb (14,000kg) B-25 Mitchell bombers in April 1942, as well as 65 of her own aircraft in the hangar, and by June 1942 all three ships were carrying 79 naval aircraft. Two years later, *Enterprise* was able to operate 78 of the heavier new types, but only by accepting a larger deck park than had been intended.

Machinery: Four sets of geared turbines were installed and in spite of a total output only 80% that of the lighter *Hiryu*, the 'Yorktown' class was barely a half-knot slower. The four boiler uptakes were trunked into a large funnel set in the island – the first combined island/funnel to appear in a US Navy carrier design.

Armament: The eight 5-in AA guns were disposed in an identical way to those of *Ranger*, with fire control directors on the island. Four 1.1-in quadruple AA guns were installed, three fore and aft of the island and one at the starboard deck edge. A few 20mm Oerlikons were installed early in 1942 and

YORKTOWN *as she apeared in 1938. Two of the forward arrester wires can be seen just abaft the forward lift (and above the forward hangar opening).*

(US NAVY)

towards the end of that year *Enterprise* was armed with quadruple 40mm Bofors in place of the 1.1-in guns; by 1944, she was carrying 40 Bofors and 50 Oerlikons. Air warning radar and IFF gear was installed in all three ships by May 1942 and in *Enterprise* this was continually up-dated and height-finding and fire-control radar added.

Fates: *Yorktown* was damaged by a 250kg (551lb) semi-armour-piercing bomb on 8 May 1942; the bomb failed to penetrate the main armoured deck and the fires started were soon brought under control. On 4 June, off Midway, she was hit by three 250kg bombs, two medium capacity bombs which exploded on contact with the flight deck and the funnel, starting fires and blowing out five of the six boilers, and an SAP bomb which started a petrol fire above the armoured deck and the magazines. The latter were promptly flooded and the petrol tanks and voids topped up with CO_2 but the ship was still on fire when she was hit by two torpedoes abreast the port wing machinery spaces. All power was lost and the ship abandoned when the list reached 26° – prematurely, for she remained afloat. Salvage was attempted on 5 and 6 June but was brought to an end when two submarine torpedoes hit her on 6th. Flooding spread and *Yorktown* foundered at around dawn on 7 June 1942.

Hornet was hit by five 250kg and two 60kg bombs, two torpedoes and two aircraft within the space of seven minutes off Santa Cruz on 26 October 1942. The carrier was set on fire and was left dead in the water with a 12½° list. She was taken in tow but six hours after the first attack she was hit by a third torpedo and sustained underwater damage from the mining effect of near-miss bombs. Nine American 21-in and four Japanese 24-in destroyer torpedoes were needed to scuttle *Hornet,* the enemy arriving on the scene shortly after the American destroyers had departed. *Hornet* was the last large US Navy carrier to be sunk.

HORNET *returns to Pearl Harbour after the April 1942 Doolittle Raid on Tokyo. Note the hangar side openings, the radar-controlled gunnery directors on the island, the quadruple 1.1-in AA guns fore and aft of the island, and the aircraft crane at the rear end of the island. CXAM radar is barely visible on the platform at the head of the tripod mast.*
(US NAVY)

'Yorktown' class

Displacement tonnage			
Standard	19,800		
Full load	27,500		
Dimensions			
Length (oa)	809ft 6in (246.7m); *Enterprise* 827ft (252m) in 1944		
Beam (wl)	83ft (25.3m)		
Draught	29ft (8.8m)		
Flight deck	781ft × 80ft (238m × 24.4m); *Enterprise* extended to 820ft (250m) in 1944		
Hangar	c 560ft × 75ft (170m × 23m)		
Lifts	3 – c48ft × 45ft (14.6m × 13.7m)		
Arrester wires	9 aft, 4 forward		
Catapults	3 – H-I: 5,500lb (2,500kg) @ 40 knots (46mph = 74kph) *Enterprise:* 2 H-IVC from 1943		
Aircraft stowage	79 (1942)		
Machinery	4 sets geared turbines; 4 shafts		
shp	120,000 (design)		
speed	32-33 knots (sea speed)		
fuel	7,487 tons		
radius	8,220nm (9,465 stm = 15,150km) at 20 knots		
Aviation fuel	155,600 Imp galls (186,860 US galls = 707,360 litres)		
	Hornet (1942)	**Enterprise** (1944)	
Armament	8×5-in (127mm) AA	8×5-in	
	4×4 1.1-in (27.94mm) AA	6×4, 8×2 40mm AA	
	23 × 20mm AA	50 × 20mm AA	
Complement	2,919 (1942)		
Builder	Newport News, Va		
	Yorktown (CV.5)	**Enterprise** (CV.6)	**Hornet** (CV.8)
Laid down	21 May 1938	16 July 1934	25 Sep 1939
Launched	4 Aprl 1936	30 Oct 1936	14 Dec 1940
Commissioned	30 Sept 1937	12 May 1938	20 Oct 1941
Sunk	7 Jun 1942	—	27 Oct 1942

USS *Wasp*

The US Navy ordered its seventh carrier in 1935. With 120,300 tons used out of the Treaty allocation of 135,000 tons for carriers, it was decided to build an 'improved *Ranger*' type, lightly armoured and with lower propulsive power, accepting a smaller aircraft complement than in the 'Yorktown' class.

A contemporary of the Royal Navy's *Illustrious*, CV.7, named *Wasp*, provides an interesting contrast in styles and apparent achievement. With a displacement about 8,000 tons less than *Illustrious*, *Wasp* had a larger usable flight deck area on a narrower hull, attained the same speed on 30% less power and operated double the number of aircraft. Against these advantages were her lack of protection, in armour and gun armament, and the fact that she carried less fuel and ordnance per aircraft than *Illustrious*.

Hull: *Wasp* was some 40ft (12.2m) shorter than *Ranger* but slightly beamier, giving her a hull waterline length:beam ratio of 8.5:1 as opposed to 9:1. The armoured belt and deck protection was basically the same as that in the earlier ship but internal sub-division was much improved.

Flight Deck and Hangar: The flight deck extended for the full length of the ship, without a pronounced round-down aft. Two H-I catapults were fitted in the flight deck and one in the hangar. Eight arrester wires aft and six forward used the same pattern of hydraulic control unit as the three barriers, the limitations of the gear and of the two centre-line lifts, being identical to those of the 'Yorktown' class. The large open-sided hangar could accommodate over 70 aircraft and she actually operated between 66 and 72 in the Pacific; in April and May 1942, she embarked British Spitfire fighters and flew off 64 of them on each occasion in two Malta ferry operations, at the same time retaining a score of her aircraft.

Machinery: Like *Ranger*, *Wasp* was a two-shaft ship, but with reduced fineness and increased draught she needed an extra 21,500hp to reach the same speed. The machinery was located amidships, unlike that of *Ranger*, and the six boiler uptakes were all trunked across to the starboard side to a single relatively small funnel set in the island.

Armament: Gun armament was the same as that in the 'Yorktown' class – eight 5-in dual-purpose guns in four deck-edge sponsons and four quadruple 1.1-in automatic AA mountings distributed fore and aft of the island. The two fire control directors were stabilised and were fitted with ranging radar at the end of 1941. At the same time, CXAM air warning and fighter control radar was installed.

Fate: *Wasp* was serving with the US Atlantic Fleet in December 1941, alongside *Yorktown* and

WASP'S *fiery end: the burning carrier is seen just after the first monstrous petrol explosion which followed the three hits scored on her starboard side by the submarine* I-19, *south of Guadalcanal, on 15 September 1942.* (US NAVY)

The reduction in number of boilers from nine to six resulted in WASP *being endowed with a smaller funnel than the 'Yorktown' class, and no other American carrier was subsequently built with such a large gap between funnel and foremast. Note triaxially-stabilised radar-equipped fire-control directors on the island, partially-opened hangar side shutters, 20mm Oerlikons in deck-edge bandstands, and CXAM radar above tripod. The photograph was taken in January 1942 after a refit at Norfolk Navy Yard.* (US NAVY)

Ranger. The two smaller ships remained and *Wasp* was attached to the British Home Fleet from March to May 1942, after the Royal Navy's modern carriers had been sent to the Indian Ocean. Joining the US Pacific Fleet after the loss of *Yorktown* at Midway, she took part in the invasion of Guadalcanal but was refuelling on the day of the Battle of the Eastern Solomons, 24 August. On 13 September 1942, *Wasp* flew off 20 US Marine Corps fighters to Guadalcanal and then remained in a small geographical area to cover ships heading for the island.

South of the Solomons, in the early afternoon of 15 September, she was hit by three torpedoes fired by the Japanese submarine *I-19*. Two hit deep on the starboard side, abreast the petrol tanks, which were split, and one very shallow, causing widespread above-water damage, including breaking the flight-deck petrol pipes and firemains. The main machinery was undamaged, but the lack of firemain pressure allowed the fires to gain ground and the fuel vapour from the damaged main tanks was detonated within minutes of the torpedo hits; secondary explosions were triggered off as the fire reached aircraft bombs, torpedoes, ammunition and aircraft fuel tanks. *Wasp* was abandoned 35 minutes after the attack and was scuttled, still blazing fiercely and suffering explosions of increasing force, an hour and a half later.

USS *Wasp*

Displacement tonnage	
Standard	14,700
Full load	20,500
Dimensions	
Length (oa)	741ft 3in (226m)
Beam (wl)	80ft 9in (24.6m)
Draught	23ft (7m)
Flight deck	c 735ft × 80ft (224 × 24.4m)
Hangar	c 500ft × 75ft (152m × 23m)
Lifts	2 – c48ft × 45ft (14.6m × 13.7m)
Arrester wires	8 aft, 6 forward
Catapults	3 – H-I (as 'Yorktown' class)
Aircraft stowage	72
Machinery	2 sets geared turbines; 2 shafts
shp	75,000 (design)
speed	29.5 knots (design)
fuel	4,353 tons
radius	c 8,000nm (9,200 stm = 14,750km) at 20 knots
Aviation fuel	91,163 Imp galls (109,480 US galls = 414,430 litres)
Armament	8 × 5-in (127mm) AA
	4 × 4 1.1-in (27.94mm) AA
	c 30 × 20mm AA
Complement	2,367
Builder	Bethlehem Steel Co (Quincy)
Laid down	1 April 1936
Launched	4 April 1939
Commissioned	25 April 1940
Sunk	15 September 1942

'Essex' class

The 'Essex' class was originally envisaged, in 1939, as a 25,000-ton improved-*Yorktown*, carrying heavier aircraft in an enlarged hangar. The design was modified and by the time that the first order for 11 of this class was placed in 1940 the displacement had been increased by 2,100 tons, due mainly to an increase in the armour and armament.

Although all 32 ships authorised in the 1940-44 Programmes were described as 'Essex class', there were in fact two types, eight ships of the first Programme and one in each of the two succeeding Programmes being of the original 872ft (265m) overall length and the remainder extended above the waterline at bow and stern to give a total length of 888ft (270m). CV.35 and 46 (*Reprisal* and *Iwo Jima*) were cancelled four days before the end of the War, while they were still on the slipway, and CV.50 to 55 had already been cancelled in March 1945, before they had been laid down. By using a completely standard main and auxiliary machinery installation in all ships and placing orders with only five yards, the building times were considerably reduced: one of the two civilian firms, Newport News Shipbuilding Co, built seven of the first eleven on four slipways between April 1941 and October 1944, the average building time being 17½ months.

Hull: As with previous American fast carriers, the 'Essex' class had a high length:beam ratio – 8.8:1. The waterline beam was less than that of the British 'Illustrious' class and the maximum beam at the flight deck appreciably greater, but, with the armour set at hangar deck and below, the big American carriers were no less steady and their greater length made them less prone to heavy pitching in the usual long Pacific swell. The main horizontal armour was on the hangar deck, where it was 2½in thick over machinery and magazines; the main deck was one and a half inches thick and extended to the ship's side, meeting the top of the 5in waterline belt. The total horizontal thickness was thus the same as that in the Royal Navy's armoured carriers, but whereas the latter intended that the hangar was the absolute last line of defence, in the 'Essex' class a heavy bomb might not be stopped until it was three decks below the hangar. Anti-torpedo protection was good and the vertical sandwiches of fuel oil and empty compartments took up 35ft (10.6m) of the underwater beam abreast the machinery spaces.

Flight Deck and Hangar: The *Essex* was the epitomy of the unaerodynamic carrier, with a cluttered island and plank-like flight deck making no concessions to improving airflow. The arrester wires (forward and aft) and the barriers were designed to stop 12,000lb aircraft, although this weight limitation was subsequently increased,

LEXINGTON, *the second unit of the superb 'Essex' class to be completed is seen here during the work up of her Air Group 94 in the late spring of 1945. Note the pyramidal island, the 'basket' antenna of the SK-2 radar at the rear of the funnel, the port-side deck-edge lift platform abreast the island, the reduced number of hangar side openings (in comparison with the 'Yorktown' class), and the five quadruple 40mm Bofors AA mountings in sponsons on the starboard side.* (US NAVY)

engaging at up to 75 knots with a shorter pull-out than contemporary British gear. Two 86½ft (26.4m) H-IV catapults were installed forward on the flight deck and a third on the hangar deck in three early ships – the last being a double-action athwartships-firing installation which was seldom used and was removed before the end of the War. The original H-IVC deck catapults, with a 16,000lb (7,270kg)/74knot limit, were replaced by 18,000lb (8,180kg)/78knot H-IVBs in later units. Three large lifts were installed, one centrally at the forward end of the hangar, one offset to starboard but within the structure just abaft the island, and the third at the port deck edge amidships, running in two heavily braced channels outside the hull. A gallery deck, for accommodation and stores stowage, was inserted between the flight deck and hangar roof, minimum overhead clearance in the hangar being 18ft (5.5m). The original 'Essex' class Air Group was established as 36 fighters, 36 scout-dive-bombers and 18 torpedo-bombers, plus one aircraft for the Air Group Commander; a year later, in July 1944, the numbers were altered to 54 – 24 – 15. Hardly had all carriers been re-armed to this scale before, in January 1945, it was altered again, to 73 – 15 – 15. In the same month, two ships operated 93 fighters and 15 torpedo-bombers for one operation only. During sustained operations, up to 30 aircraft could be flown off every two hours during daylight, so that it was barely surprising that the 12 large and seven Light carriers operating off Okinawa between 30 March and 30 April 1945 managed to launch 24,393 sorties.

Machinery: The four-shaft lay-out of the 'Yorktown' class was retained and standardisation was maintained by using Westinghouse geared turbines and Babcock & Wilcox boilers in all ships. Improved trunking and draught arrangements led to a reduction in size of the funnel, which was diminutive by comparison with that in the 'Yorktown' class. The enormous fuel oil capacity was ideal for the Pacific and the 'long-hulled' ships' range of 17,250 miles (31,780km) was unrivalled by any surface warship prior to nuclear propulsion.

Armament: The weakness of the earlier carrier classes' main AA gunnery armament was corrected in the 'Essex' class, which carried eight 5-in DP guns in twin gunhouses, two ahead of and two abaft the island, as well as four single 5-in guns located at the port deck edge. Blast damage to aircraft from the guns around the island was accepted, but the two mountings abaft the island proved to be a major obstruction to aircraft landing off-centre. Two radar-equipped directors controlled all eight mountings and the directors for the quadruple 40mm mountings, which increased in numbers from 11 to 18, were later fitted with blind-fire control; the 35 single 20mm Oerlikons around the deck-edges were doubled-up in 1944, giving the ships a total of 142 automatic AA barrels. The radar

The second WASP, *part of Task Force 38, posing for the camera two days after the War ended.*

(US NAVY)

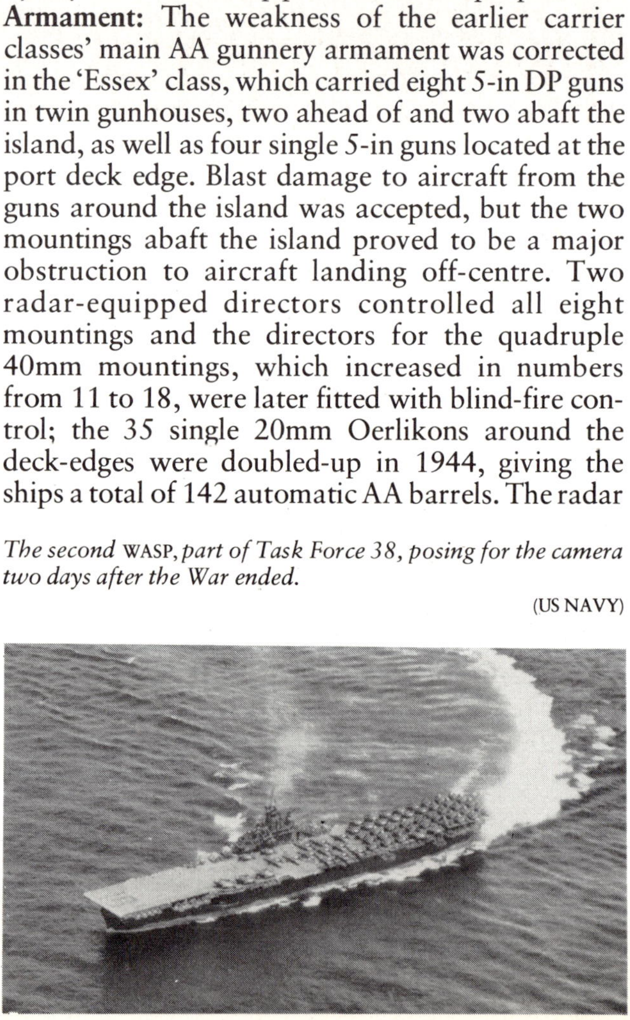

equipment was comprehensive, consisting of a long-range air warning and control set (SK) with a range of up to 120 miles, a shorter-range standby air-warning set (SC) and, from 1944, a narrow-beam height-finding set (SP) which became the primary fighter-direction set. From late 1944, the overhead 'gap' in the radar cover became a serious problem with the advent of the *Kamikazes* and several ships rigged upwards-facing aircraft radars for use as 'zenith air search' sets. IFF, radar beacons and the YE beacon were all fitted as standard and most ships had active and passive electronic countermeasures gear.

Damage: No 'Essex' class carrier was sunk, but the following were seriously damaged by enemy action:

Lexington (CV.16)	4 Dec 43	hit aft by air torpedo
Intrepid (CV.11)	17 Feb 44	hit aft by air torpedo
Franklin (CV.13)	30 Oct 44	suicide attack
Lexington (CV.16)	5 Nov 44	suicide attack
Intrepid (CV.11)	25 Nov 44	suicide attack
Ticonderoga (CV.14)	21 Jan 45	suicide attack
Randolph (CV.15)	11 March 45	suicide attack
**Franklin* (CV.13)	19 March 45	bombed
**Wasp* (CV.18)	19 March 45	bombed
Hancock (CV.19)	7 April 45	suicide attack
Intrepid (CV.11)	16 April 45	suicide attack
**Bunker Hill* (CV.17)	11 May 45	suicide attack

(*these three ships were not repaired before the end of the War)

'Essex' class – CV-9 type

Displacement tonnage	
Standard	27,100
Full load	34,200-34,800, except *Bunker Hill* 35,700
Dimensions	
Length (oa)	872ft (265.9m)
Beam (wl)	93ft (28.4m)
Draught	29ft (8.8m)
Flight deck	866ft × 90ft (109ft maximum) (264 × 27.4 – 33.2m)
Hangar	580ft × 71ft (minimum) (176.8m × 21.6m)
Lifts	3 – 2 inboard, c47ft × 47ft (14.3 × 14.3m) 1 deck-edge, 60ft (18.3m) long
Arrester wires	9 aft, 6 forward
Catapults	2 H-IVC (see *Saratoga*); 1 H-IVA (hangar installation) in *Essex, Yorktown, Bunker Hill*
Aircraft stowage	90-108 (see text)
Machinery	4 sets geared turbines; 4 shafts
shp	150,000
speed	33 knots (32 knots sustained)
fuel	c 6,300 tons (43,838 US barrels)
radius	14,100nm (16,250 stm = 26,000km) at 20 knots
Aviation fuel	192,895 Imp galls (231,650 US galls = 875,750 litres) in *Essex, Lexington, Yorktown, Intrepid;* 188,090 Imp galls (225,880 US galls = 855,060 litres) in others
Armament	4 × 2 5-in (127mm) DP, 4 × 1 5-in AA 17 × 4 40mm AA 35 × 2 20mm AA
Complement	3,448

'Essex' class – CV.14 (long-hulled) type

As CV.9 type, except:

Displacement tonnage	
Full load	c 36,000
Dimensions	
Length (oa)	888ft (270.66m)
Flight deck	870ft (265.2m) length
Catapults	2 × H-IVC; later units 2 × H-IVB (see text)
Machinery	
fuel	c 6,650 tons (*Hancock* and *Ticonderoga* as CV.9 type)
radius	17,250nm (19,860 stm = 31,780km) at 20 knots
Aviation fuel	*Hancock* and *Ticonderoga* 188,090 Imp galls; *Randolph* 202,080 Imp galls (242,684 US galls = 918,670 litres); others 174,740 Imp galls (209,850 US galls = 794,362 litres)
Armament	12 × 5in 18 × 40mm AA 35 × 2 20mm
Complement	3,454

'Essex' class

	Builder	Bldg Time (mths)	Commissioned
Essex (CV.9)	Newport News	20	31 Dec 1942
Lexington (CV.16)	Bethlehem	20½	17 March 1943
Yorktown (CV.10)	Newport News	16½	15 May 1943
Bunker Hill (CV.17)	Bethlehem	20½	24 May 1943
Intrepid (CV.11)	Newport News	20½	16 Aug 1943
Wasp (CV.18)	Bethlehem	20	24 Nov 1943
Hornet (CV.12)	Newport News	16	29 Nov 1943
Franklin (CV.13)	Newport News	14	31 Jan 1944
**Hancock* (CV.19)	Bethlehem	14½	15 April 1944
**Ticonderoga* (CV.14)	Newport News	15	8 May 1944
Bennington (CV.20)	New York NY	21	6 Aug 1944
**Shangri-La* (CV.38)	Norfolk NY	21½	15 Sept 1944
**Randolph* (CV.15)	Newport News	17	9 Oct 1944
Bon Homme Richard (CV.31)	New York NY	23	26 Nov 1944
**Antietam* (CV.36)	Philadelphia NY	23½	28 Jan 1945
**Boxer* (CV.21)	Newport News	19	16 April 1945
**Lake Champlain* (CV.39)	Norfolk NY	26½	3 June 1945

The following were completed after the end of the War: (1945) *Princeton* (CV.37), *Tarawa* (CV.40); (1946) *Leyte* (CV.32), *Kearsarge* (CV.33), *Valley Forge* (CV.45), *Philippine Sea* (CV.47); *Oriskany* (CV.34) completed in much-modified form in 1950, 77 months after she was laid down.

(*indicates 'long-hulled' type)

'Independence' class

In March 1942 the US Navy ordered the conversion of nine light cruiser hulls as emergency-type fast carriers. No fewer than 36 of the 'Cleveland' class cruisers had been ordered in 1940 and 1941 and with a tonnage of 10,000 (standard) and a length of 600ft (183m) on the waterline, they were believed to be the smallest hulls that could be adapted to give a useful aircraft capacity with fleet speed. Five ships had already been laid down and of these three were commissioned by the end of March 1943. All were built by New York Shipbuilding Co, which also completed five of the first cruisers on the original order.

Hull: The light cruiser hull was completed up to the fo'c'sle deck, the interior being modified to incorporate extra accommodation, bomb magazines, aviation stores and aviation fuel stowage. The standard displacement rose from 10,000 to 11,000 tons, much of which was above the fo'c'sle, and to preserve the stability bulges had to be added below the waterline, increasing the beam by five feet (1.5m) and so reducing the length:beam ratio to 8.4:1 from 9:1; deep draught increased by 12 inches. The deck armour varied in thickness between two and three inches, distributed over the hangar and armoured decks, and the main belt was two inches thick, increasing to five inches (127mm) outboard of magazines. The belt was omitted in *Independence* and *Princeton,* possibly in order to keep the weight within the specified limits.

Flight Deck and Hangar: The 552ft wooden flight deck formed the roof of the hangar and was not extended right to the bows. Two H-IVC catapults were installed right forward and with eight arrester wires of the same pattern as those in *Essex,* the 'Light carriers' could operate aircraft up to the same weights as those in the bigger carrier. Both of the lifts were on the centre-line, no deck edge position being practical. The hangar was a major source of disappointment when the first ship arrived at San Francisco: with a length of only 215ft (65.5m) and a breadth of 58ft (17.6m), it was smaller than that in the 'Sangamon' class converted oilers and quite inadequate for the specified complement of 24 fighters, 12 dive-bombers and nine torpedo-bombers. *Independence* and *Princeton* began their work-up with this complement, but when the Grumman Hellcat replaced the Wildcat as the fast carrier fighter, the Light carrier Air Groups were adjusted by the elimination of the dive-bombers. There was pressure from the Fleet for the removal of the torpedo-bombers but this was resisted and it was not until just before the end of the War that it was approved to equip the Light carriers entirely with fighters, 36 Hellcats or Vought Corsairs.

The small island also came in for criticism, mainly due to its lack of accommodation, but there was little that could be done to improve it and the commanders came to accept the limitations.

Machinery: The 'Cleveland' class main machinery was retained, geared turbines producing 100,000hp to drive four shafts. Performance was not particularly impressive for at normal displacement (14,000 tons) *Independence* could reach only 31.6 knots and later ships just over 31 knots, so that they were appreciably slower than the 'Essex' class. Radius of action was half that of the big carriers but considerably better than that of their light cruiser half-cousins. The four boilers were separately ducted to

View of the midships and aft section of USS INDEPENDENCE *in July 1943, six weeks before she first went into action and before the Dauntless dive-bomber squadron was disembarked. Note the decking extending right up to the four angled funnels and the port-side extension to permit the transfer of aircraft around the forward lift area, the SK-1 radar on its pedestal immediately ahead of No 3 funnel, the crane forward of the island, and the five twin 40mm mountings along the port deck edge.* ▼ (US NAVY)

INDEPENDENCE, *the first designated 'Night carrier', seen with TF38 during operations off Formosa in mid-October 1944; Grumman F6F-3N night-fighters and TBM-1E Avenger torpedo-bombers are ranged in readiness for the night's operations.* ▼ (US NAVY)

MONTEREY'S *light cruiser hull creates remarkably little water disturbance at near maximum speed. The supporting braces under the island and funnels carry the obstruction well clear to starboard of the deck. The three dark stripes inboard of No 2 funnel are the lowered barriers.* (US NAVY)

small funnels located at the starboard flight deck edge. The funnels were fixed in the upright position but being only about 14ft tall (4.25m) they constituted no great hazard, apart from the fact that they did not carry the smoke as far away from the deck as a normal tall stack on an island or even the Japanese-style downward-facing funnel.

Armament: A single open 5-in DP gun was carried on a sponson over the stern of the first four ships of the class, but this position was occupied by a quadruple 40mm in the remainder and when the 5-in was removed from the early ships the standard armament for the class consisted of two quadruple 40mm (one at bow and stern), nine twin 40mm and five twin 20mm mountings (six in *Monterey*) disposed around the edge of the flight deck. SK and SC radar was fitted, the former on a stump mast just ahead of the third funnel, as well as the usual homing and radar beacons and navigational radar; no height-finding radar could be fitted due partly to topweight considerations and also to lack of mast space.

Loss: The only ship lost was *Princeton* (CVL.23), which was hit by a single 250kg (551lb) semi-armour-piercing bomb dropped by a Japanese dive-bomber off Luzon on 24 October 1944. The bomb passed through the flight and hangar decks and detonated on the main armour deck, starting a severe fire. This spread to the hangar, where six fully-fuelled aircraft intensified the blaze. The between-decks ventilation intakes were in the hangar and the smoke and heat spread throughout the ship, forcing her abandonment 40 minutes after the hit, only the fire-fighting parties remaining, backed up by ships lying alongside to play hoses on the fires. By mid-afternoon, it appeared that there was a chance of saving the carrier, but then the torpedo warheads 'cooked-off' with an enormous explosion, wrecking the carrier and inflicting serious damage on the light cruiser *Birmingham* alongside. *Princeton* was then scuttled by torpedoing.

'Independence' class

Displacement tonnage	
Standard	11,000
Full load	14,300 (except *Independence* and *Princeton* 14,000)
Dimensions	
Length (oa)	622ft 6in (189.8m)
Beam (bulges)	71ft 6in (21.8m)
Draught	26ft (7.9m)
Flight deck	525ft × 73ft (max width 109ft 6in) (160.1m × 22.25 – 33.4m)
Hangar	215ft × 58ft (65.5m × 17.6m)
Lifts	2 – 43ft × 42ft (13.1m × 12.8m)
Arrester wires	8 (aft)
Catapults	2 H-IVC (see *Saratoga*)
Aircraft stowage	31 (see text)
Machinery	4 sets geared turbines; 4 shafts
shp	100,000
fuel	c 2,460 tons (17,214 US barrels)
radius	7,600nm (8,750 stm = 14,000km) at 20 knots
Aviation fuel	101,800 Imp galls (122,243 US galls = 462,745 litres)
Armament (1944)	2 × 4, 9 × 2 40mm AA 5 × 2 20mm (*Monterey* 6 × 2 20mm)
Complement	1,569

'Independence' class

All built by the New York Shipbuilding Co, the first five being laid down as 'Cleveland' class light cruisers

	Launched	**Commissioned**
Independence (CVL.22, ex-CL.59)	22 August 1942	14 January 1943
Princeton (CVL.23, ex-CL.61)	17 October 1942	25 February 1943
Belleau Wood (CVL.24, ex-CL.76)	6 December 1942	31 March 1943
Cowpens (CVL.25, ex-CL.77)	17 January 1943	28 May 1943
Monterey (CLV.26, ex-CL.78)	28 February 1943	17 June 1943
	Building Time (months)	**Commissioned**
Cabot (CVL.28, ex-CL.79)	16	24 July 1943
Langley (CVL.27, ex-CL.85)	16½	31 August 1943
Bataan (CVL.29, ex-CL.99)	15½	17 November 1943
San Jacinto (CVL.30, ex-CL.100)	13½	15 December 1943

Had the War continued into 1946, the US Fast Carrier Striking Force would have been reinforced by the three 'Battle Carriers' of the 'Midway class', the first two of which, MIDWAY *and* FRANKLIN D ROOSEVELT *(illustrated), commissioned in October 1945. Note the armoured flight deck, the removal of all 5-in DP guns to deck-edge galleries, the outboard lift, and the 82 Vought F4U Corsairs and Curtiss SB2C Helldivers parked on deck.*
(US NAVY)